At Issue

Casualties of War

Other Books in the At Issue Series:

Anorexia

Are America's Wealthy Too Powerful?

Are Social Networking Sites Harmful?

Campaign Finance

Cell Phones and Driving

Child Labor Sweatshops

Do Children Have Rights?

The H1N1 Flu

Is Childhood Becoming Too Sexualized?

Is Torture Ever Justified?

Racial Profiling

Should Character Be Taught in School?

Should the U.S. Reduce Its Consumption?

Teen Sex

Transgender People

Uranium Mining

U.S. Military Deployment

Wave and Tidal Power

What Is the Impact of Emigration?

Women in Islam

At Issue

Casualties of War

Susan Hunnicutt, Book Editor

GREENHAVEN PRESS
A part of Gale, Cengage Learning

 GALE
CENGAGE Learning·

Detroit • New York • San Francisco • New Haven, Conn • Waterville, Maine • London

Christine Nasso, *Publisher*
Elizabeth Des Chenes, *Managing Editor*

© 2011 Greenhaven Press, a part of Gale, Cengage Learning.

Gale and Greenhaven Press are registered trademarks used herein under license.

For more information, contact:
Greenhaven Press
27500 Drake Rd.
Farmington Hills, MI 48331-3535
Or you can visit our Internet site at http://www.gale.cengage.com

For product information and technology assistance, contact us at

Gale Customer Support, 1-800-877-4253
For permission to use material from this text or product, submit all requests online at
www.cengage.com/permissions

Further permissions questions can be emailed to permissionrequest@cengage.com

Articles in Greenhaven Press anthologies are often edited for length to meet page requirements. In addition, original titles of these works are changed to clearly present the main thesis and to explicitly indicate the author's opinion. Every effort is made to ensure that Greenhaven Press accurately reflects the original intent of the authors. Every effort has been made to trace the owners of copyrighted material.

Cover image © Images.com/Corbis.

LIBRARY OF CONGRESS CATALOGING-IN-PUBLICATION DATA

Casualties of war / Susan Hunnicutt, book editor.
    p. cm. -- (At issue)
    Includes bibliographical references and index.
    ISBN 978-0-7377-4880-2 (hardcover)
    ISBN 978-0-7377-4881-9 (pbk.)
    1. Iraq War, 2003---Casualties--Juvenile literature. 2. Afghan War, 2001---Casualties--Juvenile literature. I. Hunnicutt, Susan.
    DS79.767.C37C36 2011
    956.7044'3--dc22
                                                                    2010037582

Printed in the United States of America
2 3 4 5 6 7 14 13 12 11

Contents

Introduction   **7**

1. Americans Are Insensitive to the Human Costs   **11**
   of War
   Michael Tennant

2. Many Soldier Casualties of the Iraq/Afghanistan   **16**
   Wars Go Uncounted
   Aaron Glantz

3. Casualties in Afghanistan Demand War Rationale   **19**
   Be Publicly Debated
   Stewart Nusbaumer

4. Civilian Deaths Undermine Allied Security   **24**
   Efforts in Afghanistan
   Human Rights Watch

5. U.S. Casualties in Iraq Are Not Comparable to   **29**
   Those in Vietnam
   Tim Kane and David D. Gentilli

6. U.S. Contractors in Iraq Are Hidden Casualties   **34**
   of the War
   T. Christian Miller

7. Iraqi Military Interpreters Must Fight for   **43**
   Compensation for Injuries
   Dubai News.Net

8. Media Coverage of Returning Fallen Soldiers Is   **47**
   To Be Allowed Again
   Editor & Publisher

9. Media Coverage of Fallen Soldiers Is Not   **51**
   Transparent Enough
   Kevin Baron

10. Media Interest in Covering the Return of Fallen   **56**
Soldiers Has Fallen
Matt Towery

11. The Costs of Caring for U.S. War Casualties Are   **60**
Enormous
Andrew Stephen

12. The Military Is Losing Ground in Its Battle   **70**
Against Soldier Suicides
Halimah Abdullah

13. The Military Response to Soldiers Experiencing   **75**
Stress Is Changing
Richard Mauer

14. Condolences Should Go to Families of Soldiers   **87**
Who Commit Suicide
Michael Blumenfield

15. Condolences Should Not Go to Families of   **91**
Soldiers Who Commit Suicide
Paul Steinberg

16. Casualties of the War on Terror Have Made a   **94**
Military Welfare State
Gordon Duff

17. Casualties from Terrorism Are Minor   **98**
Compared to Other Threats
Tom Englehardt

Organizations to Contact   **107**

Bibliography   **113**

Index   **118**

Introduction

When Warren Hardy came home his family could tell that something was wrong. "You see pictures of soldiers. . . reuniting with the families and . . . everything is great," his wife says in an interview with Bob Woodruff for *Nightline*. "We didn't have that kind of reunion. When I saw him for the first time, I was disappointed. He was just different, and I couldn't understand why."[1]

Hardy, who is a decorated veteran, served with the First Armored Division in Iraq. A few months into his tour of duty in 2004, the vehicle he was riding in was hit by a land mine near Tikrit, and thrown more than 10 feet into the air. Hardy survived the explosion and was sent to a combat hospital where he was treated for knee injuries. Two days later, he was back on patrol. Soon, however, he began to feel that something was not right. "I was always banging my head against obstacles," Hardy says. "My memory of what's around me wasn't keeping the information. . . I just didn't feel as smart."

The full extent of Hardy's cognitive difficulties did not become apparent until after his return to the United States. Before serving in Iraq he had worked as a software engineer. Now Hardy found it difficult to concentrate. "Nothing sunk in," he said. "The harder I tried, the more frustrated I got. . . I had an incredible memory, and now I am struggling." Eventually Hardy, who is the father of four small children, was diagnosed with a traumatic brain injury (TBI), a physical wound that is often invisible, caused by shockwaves associated with bomb explosions that tear brain cells apart. Some health professionals have identified traumatic brain injuries caused by improvised explosive devices—IEDs—as signature injuries of

---

1. Bob Woodruff and Jim Hill, "'Something Was Different.' Vet Copes with Invisible Injury: Iraq Veteran Warren Hardy Suffers From an Undiagnosed Traumatic Brain Injury," ABC News/Nightline, March 7, 2007.

the Iraq war. It is possible, however, for TBI to go undiagnosed at the time of injury and to be left untreated for many months and even years. Persistent symptoms—including headache, sleep disturbance, irritability, dizziness, imbalance, fatigue, inattention, and problems with concentration or memory—can have a significant effect on an individual's ability to work. Coping with the impact of undiagnosed injuries can leave families emotionally stressed and financially vulnerable.

In the early days of the wars in Iraq and Afghanistan, between October 2001 and January 2007, the Defense and Veterans Brain Injury Center documented only 2,121 cases of TBI. However, some neurologists contend that that cases of traumatic brain injuries from that time were greatly underreported because only penetrative head injuries were counted. They believe that the actual incidence of TBI among returning veterans was probably much higher, and that many veterans were returning home with untreated injuries. Reacting to these concerns, the United States Congress in 2007 and 2008 appropriated nearly $1 billion for brain-injury research and treatment. Comprehensive screenings carried out by the military have since revealed that between 10 and 20 percent of personnel who have served in Iraq have suffered concussions. In 2009 the Pentagon released a report acknowledging that as many as 360,000 veterans of Iraq and Afghanistan may have suffered from traumatic brain injuries.

Despite increased levels of funding for research, screening and treatment, controversy continues to gather around the question of whether TBI is being properly diagnosed, and whether those who are suffering from this disorder are receiving the appropriate care. A 2010 investigation carried out by ProPublica, a non-profit news organization, found that despite public interest and attention, military doctors and screening systems continue to miss brain trauma in soldiers. Even when head injuries are correctly diagnosed in the field, the information often is not preserved. Handheld devices designed to store and transmit electronic health records have proven undependable in war zones, while paper records have sometimes been lost.

At the same time, others have questioned whether it is even helpful to diagnose mild cases of TBI. An April 2009 article published in the *New England Journal of Medicine* criticized recently-adopted measures for identifying concussion injuries, arguing that these guidelines are subjective and that they can lead to misdiagnosis and unnecessary treatment. "The clinical definition of 'concussion/mild TBI' . . . is inadequate," wrote Dr. Charles W. Hoge, who served as director of the Division of Psychiatry and Neuroscience in the Battlemind Training office at Walter Reed Army Institute of Research in 2009. Hoge and his co-authors believe that complete recovery from concussions that are less serious is quite common. They also state that media attention surrounding traumatic brain injuries in returning veterans has clouded the treatment picture in such cases. "Widespread use of the terms 'mild TBI,' 'signature injury,' 'invisible wound,' and 'silent epidemic,' as well as patient-education materials that combine mild TBI with more serious types of TBI, are examples of poor risk communication," the article in the *New England Journal of Medicine* states. "The perspective that mild TBI is part of a medical continuum with moderate and severe TBI guides interventions, despite strong evidence that they are distinct clinically and epidemiologically."

Service men and women who have been wounded in battle depend on health professionals in the field to accurately identify the injuries they have suffered and to prescribe appropriate treatment. After these veterans return home, they continue to depend on medical professionals with the Department of Defense and the Veterans Administration to accurately identify the extent of disability and prescribe levels of care. These decisions can impact the lives of service men and women and their families for years into the future. How can the Veterans Administration and the Department of Defense improve their practices of caring for those who have been injured in battle? This is one of the questions that is considered in *At Issue: Casualties of War.*

1

Americans Are Insensitive to the Human Costs of War

Michael Tennant

Michael Tennant is a software developer and writer who lives in Pittsburgh, Pennsylvania.

With the help of technology and gratuitous media violence, American society has become largely removed from the real bloodshed, carnage and human cost of wars in Iraq, Afghanistan and other places. Americans will allow violence and loss of life to go on indefinitely, as long as they are not touched by it in a personal way.

> *"It is well that war is so terrible; we should grow too fond of it!"*
>
> *- Gen. Robert E. Lee*

In the *Star Trek* episode "A Taste of Armageddon," Capt. James T. Kirk and crew beam down to planet Eminiar VII against the wishes of its government to find what appears to be a peaceful, highly advanced civilization. In reality, however, the planet has been at war with a nearby planet for over 500 years, suffering the loss of up to 3 million inhabitants annually. They have managed to continue functioning as a society by conducting their war entirely by computer. The computer on one planet fires virtual salvos at the other planet, whose computer in turn selects individuals who have been deemed casualties of the war. Those individuals are then ordered to report to disintegration chambers, whereupon they are vaporized. The citizens of both planets seem to accept this as their patriotic duty, for they do indeed report to the disintegration chambers when so ordered. In this way the bloodlust of both planets' governments is satisfied while their civilizations are spared the destruction caused by bombs and bullets and are therefore able to maintain the veneer of civil society.

An Immoral State of Affairs

Kirk and crew—even the highly logical Mr. Spock—immediately recognize the situation's moral repugnance. Senselessly and bloodlessly killing people on the orders of a machine, making possible a war lasting half a millennium, is no way for a supposedly civilized people to act. Says Kirk to Anan 7, the leader of the Eminiar council:

> *"Death, destruction, disease, horror: that's what war is all about, Anan. That's what makes it a thing to be avoided. But you've made it neat and painless—so neat and painless you've had no reason to stop it, and you've had it for 500 years. Since it seems to be the only way I can save my crew [declared dead by the war computer and slated for annihilation] and my ship, I'm going to end it for you—one way or another."*

Kirk's way of ending the war is to destroy the war computers, thus forcing the two planets either to begin fighting a real war or to sue for peace. Wisely, they choose the latter.

I never saw any bodies, so I could simply pretend they didn't exist.

This episode, first telecast in 1967, during a very real war in Vietnam, likely seemed farfetched at the time. While we haven't yet arrived at the stage of conducting wars completely by computer, at least from an American perspective we are far closer to it today than we were back when William Shatner was thin and Leonard Nimoy didn't have arthritis.

The Bombing of Baghdad Made Me Proud

I well recall the sense of pride I felt back during the first Gulf War in 1991 as I sat in front of my TV set, watching bombs fall from U.S. fighter jets onto buildings in Baghdad, not from cameras positioned at a distance from the bombing but from those *right inside the planes!* The visiting team was clobbering the home team on the home team's own turf! As a conservative Republican at the time, deaths of Iraqis didn't concern me in the least—they deserved it for not ousting Saddam Hussein, after all—and besides, I never saw any bodies, so I could simply pretend they didn't exist. Hardly any Americans—the only ones who really counted, anyway—were killed, and I never saw those bodies either. Anyone who bothered to point out the death and destruction being wrought upon Iraq was, as far as I was concerned, an anti-American leftist who could be safely ignored. Apparently a large majority of Americans shared my opinion: President George H.W. Bush's approval ratings shot to a record high of 89 percent.

Not for nothing is that war sometimes called the "computer war." Computers guided many of the missiles and bombs rained down upon innocent Iraqis. Meanwhile, for those of us keeping score at home, the technology employed by the military and the broadcast media allowed us to watch the Big Game live from the comfort of our couches, cheering on our team while not having our mental images of glorious victory stained with the blood of its victims.

The culture at large encourages this uninterested approach. Movies and TV shows continually up the ante on how much violence can safely be depicted.

Today we are even more detached from the horrors of war than we were in 1991. Fighter jets can be dispatched from military installations inside the U.S. to bomb distant countries. Unmanned drones kill people, regardless of their guilt or innocence, in Afghanistan and Pakistan while those controlling them enjoy the balmy climate of Florida, in danger of little more than sunburn. Few photographs of bombed-out neighborhoods or war-ravaged bodies appear in mainstream media outlets. President George W. Bush prohibits pictures of the flag-draped coffins of dead U.S. servicemen, and then, when President Barack Obama lifts the ban, the media can't be bothered even to take the pictures because they're so enamored of Obama and desperately trying to spin the ongoing wars in his favor.

At the same time, the culture at large encourages this uninterested approach. Movies and TV shows continually up the ante on how much violence can safely be depicted. Video games in which virtual humans are murdered in the goriest ways possible enthrall our youth. Having become so desensitized to violence when it's employed against the "right" people as defined by our culture and political system—after all, deaths in movies and video games aren't real, so what harm is there?—we find it easy to accept the long-distance homicide of blips on a monitor, especially when we don't even have to see those blips, let alone consider that they are living, breathing humans with the same right to life that our soldiers are allegedly defending on our behalf. Why do you think the U.S. military uses violent video games as a recruitment tool?

War Does Not Touch Us

The U.S. has been at war with Iraq to one degree or another for nearly two decades now. We've been fighting in Afghanistan for over eight years. We've conducted military incursions into Grenada, Panama, Somalia, the former Yugoslavia, and many other countries in the past 30 years. We have had troops engaged in a standoff in Korea since *I Love Lucy* was the number-one program on television. Have you noticed any of this? Has it genuinely affected the way you go about your daily life?

If you're like most Americans, your answer is *no*. Unless you've known someone in the military who was deployed to one of these conflicts (particularly if that person was wounded or killed), you've most likely gone on about your business with little awareness of the horrors being visited by and upon American soldiers and sailors. Occasionally, if something really spectacular—or horrible, depending on your point of view—hits the news wires, you may be reminded that there's a war going on, but you will quickly be returned to your regularly scheduled ignorance. Like the people of the two warring planets on *Star Trek*, as long as your way of life is not impinged upon by the war, you are perfectly happy to let it continue for decades, if not centuries.

Unless you've known someone in the military who was deployed to one of these conflicts... you've most likely gone on about your business with little awareness of the horrors being visited by and upon American soldiers.

In fact, the only thing that may prevent the U.S. from being at war until the year 2525 is economic reality. Even if we could put our own version of Kirk's plan into action, forcing our servicemen to engage the enemy in person, our government chooses to fight such tenth-rate powers that the harm they could inflict on our soldiers and our own territory is so minuscule as to have little effect on Americans' attitudes toward war. On the other hand, a collapse of our economy, which is quite foreseeable even now, will force an end to our seemingly eternal war with Eurasia, Eastasia, and every other enemy our government has dreamed up for us. The cost of empire has brought down every other great power. What makes us think it will not be our undoing?

2

Many Soldier Casualties of the Iraq/Afghanistan Wars Go Uncounted

Aaron Glantz

Aaron Glantz is the author of two books on Iraq: The War Comes Home: Washington's Battle Against America's Veterans *and* Winter Soldier: Iraq and Afghanistan: Eyewitness Accounts of the Occupations.

Many names are missing from the Pentagon's official list of casualties of the wars in Iraq and Afghanistan. For example, the victims of the Fort Hood shooting are not counted. Also absent are those American soldiers and veterans who have committed suicide after returning from the war, or those who have died as a result of self-destructive behavior due to post-traumatic stress disorder. It is important for Americans to be aware of all casualties of war, and not just those that take place while troops are deployed on foreign soil.

Perhaps the most depressing aspect of Thursday's [November 5, 2009] shoot-out at Fort Hood is that none of the 12 people who died in the melee will be counted as casualties of the wars in Iraq and Afghanistan. These soldiers—"brave Americans," President Obama called them—will join an unknown number of American soldiers, airmen, sailors and marines, who are not among the 5,267 the Defense Department counts as having died in our most recent wars, but who have perished nonetheless.

It will take days or weeks to learn what really happened at Fort Hood and why, but even at this early moment, we can make one statement for certain. The government's refusal to accurately count their sacrifice of these young men and women dishonors not only these soldiers' memories, but also obscures the public's understanding of the amount of sacrifice required to continue wars in two countries, simultaneously, overseas.

Go on the website, icasualties.org, which regularly publishes the names the Pentagon reports as having died in two wars, and a discerning eye will see a lot of other names are missing.

In January 2009, more American soldiers committed suicide than died in combat in Iraq and Afghanistan combined, but none of these deaths are listed in the official casualty count.

Many Casualties Are Not Counted

Missing are the names of service members, like Sgt. Gerald Cassidy, First Warrant Officer Judson E. Mount, or Spc. Franklin D. Barnett who died stateside after receiving substandard medical care for wounds sustained in the war zones. Cassidy sat dead in a chair for three days at Fort Knox before anyone noticed that he had passed away from complications related to a brain injury sustained in Iraq. Mount died in April 2009 at San Antonio's Brooke Army Medical Center after taking shrapnel from a roadside bomb in November 2008. Barnett died in June 2009 from wounds he sustained in Afghanistan earlier in the year.

Missing, too, are the names of American soldiers and veterans who have killed themselves after serving a tour in Iraq or Afghanistan, people like 19 year old Spc. John Fish of Paso Robles, California who told his superiors he was thinking of killing himself after his first deployment, but was ordered overseas a second time anyway. While he was training for that second deployment to Afghanistan, Fish walked out into the New Mexican desert after a training exercise for his second deployment and blew his brains out with a military issued machine gun. Or Sgt. Brian Jason Rand of North Carolina, who was found under the Cumberland River Center Pavilion near Fort Campbell, Kentucky, in February 2008 with a bullet through his skull and a shotgun by his side.

The Army reports 117 active duty Army soldiers killed themselves in 2007, the year Fish took his life. At the time, it was a 26-year high. But that record was quickly eclipsed by the 2008 Army figure of 128 suicides. In January 2009, more American soldiers committed suicide than died in combat in Iraq and Afghanistan combined, but none of these deaths are listed in the official casualty count.

Neither are the dozens of soldiers who have been killed in altercations with law enforcement brought on by Post-Traumatic Stress Disorder incurred during deployments over-seas—people like 19 year old Marine Corps veteran Andes Raya who was shot dead by police in California's rural Central Valley after returning home from Fallujah; or Minnesota Iraq war veteran Brian William Skold, who got drunk and then lead deputies on a late-night chase before stepping out of his pick-up, firing a birdshot into the air, before kneeling on one knee and leveling his shotgun at authorities. Moments later he was fatally shot by two police officers. It's unknown how many Iraq and Afghanistan war veterans have died this way, but like the 12 soldiers gunned down at Fort Hood this week, their deaths would not have occurred if not for the wars in Iraq and Afghanistan.

Regardless of what you think of these wars, it's absolutely necessary that the American public be fully appraised of their cost. After all, how can we even begin to honor their memories, if we don't even track their sacrifice.

3

Casualties in Afghanistan Demand War Rationale Be Publicly Debated

Stewart Nusbaumer

Stewart Nusbaumer served in the U.S. Marine Corps in Vietnam and later graduated from Vassar College. He is a journalist who has reported on several topics, including stories of war, from more than 100 countries.

The U.S. has not engaged in the kind of careful debate that is necessary, and that must take place, in order to justify the cost of the war in Afghanistan. The failure to talk through the reasons for U.S. involvement in Afghanistan, while continuing to put so many lives at risk, puts democracy at risk.

This press release was just issued by the US military in Afghanistan:

> KABUL, Afghanistan (October 27)—Eight U.S. service members and an Afghan civilian working with ISAF were killed today in multiple complex IED attacks in southern Afghanistan. Additionally, several service members were wounded in these incidents and were transported to a regional medical facility for treatment.

And I ask myself, why are we in Afghanistan? What is our goal there? If our troops remain in that increasingly violent country, do we need more US troops? Do we need less US

Stewart Nusbaumer, "Wait! First a Good Argument About Afghanistan!" *Huffington Post*, October 27, 2009. Reproduced by permission of the author.

troops? Maybe we have the correct number? What should be their mission? What is the mission of our country and military in the world? As you can see, I'm confused. The Taliban did not kill Americans, so why are we fighting them? They did help al Qaeda, right? I'm becoming more confused. Yet, I shouldn't be confused.

Why Are We In Afghanistan?

Recently I spent five long grueling months in Afghanistan. I studied the country up-close, traveled all over the rugged terrain, met Taliban and lots of US Marines and soldiers and civilians, and I wrote about the conflict. Still, I'm confused.

So I ask, where is the debate here at home? The national discussion leading to insights and understanding about the situation in Afghanistan and what the US role should be in that bloody country? Instead, all I hear are angry screams and empty words. All I see is a heavy fog that blankets the question: more, less, or same number of troops?

Most Americans are pretty much in the dark, and being in the dark, are unable to make a real decision. A decision they are really comfortable with making.

Our country has either lost or never possessed the capability to conduct a national discussion. With the current debate to increase or not increase the number of US troops in Afghanistan, one side is demanding we immediately make the decision and the Obama Administration is saying—well, nothing actually. Nothing in public, that is. They are doing all their real talking behind closed doors.

Some Americans are leaning in one or another direction but maintain an open mind, others are perplexed why we are in Afghanistan, still others are annoyed our mission has changed in Afghanistan—they *feel* it has changed. Still, most Americans are pretty much in the dark, and being in the dark, are unable to make a real decision. A decision they are really comfortable with making.

We Need to Talk About Our Choices

What we need is an intense, comprehensive national discussion without the stupid screaming to hurry up and make the decision and without the reassuring words from Washington that they will make the right decision. We need a genuine *public* debate!

We need the national dialogue our Founding Fathers wrote was crucial for a democracy. A vigorous debate in the marketplace of ideas that every guardian of the "people's will" insists is crucial. Instead, our media only gives us screams from the political right and reassuring words from the administration; that we are looking weak and that they will make the correct decision. Not good enough, by a long way.

When our grand experiment in democracy was launched in the 18th century, delay in decision-making was considered crucial. Big mistakes happen when decisions are made too quickly. Checks and balances were built into the heart of the system. Different branches were constructed to slow down the time-table for making decisions. Media as a forum for national debate was written into the Constitution. Slow, public discussion was considered imperative.

Today, if those who demand an instant decision believe democracy is no longer practical in the modern era, they should come out and say that *only* dictatorship or oligarchy is practical in the modern era. But these critics of our Founding Fathers refuse to say democracy is obsolete. Instead we hear shouts for a quick decision and vague words we will make the correct decision.

Leaving the Constitutional Convention in Philadelphia, Benjamin Franklin was asked what form of government the delegates were creating for the new country. He is reported to have said: "A Republic—if you can keep it!" True, if we can keep it.

"A Republic - If You Can Keep It!"

Those who want to take away democracy come in all shapes and colors. As believers of autocratic governments who hide behind the shield of national emergencies . . . as democrats who believe the democratic process is obsolete . . . as freedom-screamers in a mad rush to give freedom away . . . as idealists insisting regular citizens cannot decide important matters of state . . . as elitists insisting only they can make the decisions. And of course, the media, which only reports the shouts from the political right and the reassuring words from the administration.

[Soldiers] could be wounded or killed for a bad cause, or for a good cause with a deficient strategy. And it will leave our democracy vulnerable.

If Afghanistan is in such dire straits that we have to rush over more troops—I don't believe the prior increase in troops have all arrived in-country—then it may be time to activate the military draft and impose a war tax on Americans and American business. If we had a real debate in America, these and other issues would be under the spotlight instead of off the table. If we had a forceful, healthy national debate worthy of a strong democracy.

This is what democracy is all about. Not quick decisions. Not decisions behind closed doors. But a thorough national debate that leads to a national decision. Anything less, in this situation, will leave our combat troops vulnerable. They could be wounded or killed for a bad cause, or for a good cause with a deficient strategy. And it will leave our democracy vulnerable. Increasingly vulnerable to being circumvented and warped and eventually killed.

There is a time to talk and there is a time to act. Right now it is time to talk about what we are doing in Afghanistan and what we should do. It will be talk that is not sexy, not flashy, not decisive, but talk that is crucial for a functioning democracy. Then we need to act with the conviction of our solid understanding. One month, maybe a couple of months of discussion, and the fog of confusion should have dissipated. And then we can act.

This is how our democratic system was designed. And this is what our troops in Afghanistan deserve.

Civilian Deaths Undermine Allied Security Efforts in Afghanistan

Human Rights Watch

Human Rights Watch is an international organization that investigates allegations of human rights violations. It conducts targeted advocacy to focus attention on situations where human rights abuses have occurred.

A report released by Human Rights Watch concludes that civilian casualties resulting from U.S. and NATO air strikes are provoking a public backlash against their security forces in Afghanistan. Most civilian casualties occur during unplanned air strikes that develop as a result of emergency situations encountered by troops on the ground. Lack of troops is often a contributing factor leading to the decision to carry out an air attack.

Civilian deaths in Afghanistan from US and NATO [National Atlantic Treaty Organization] airstrikes nearly tripled from 2006 to 2007, with recent deadly airstrikes exacerbating the problem and fuelling a public backlash, Human Rights Watch said in a new report released today [September 8, 2008]. The report also condemns the Taliban's use of "human shields" in violation of the laws of war.

Though operational changes advocated by Human Rights Watch have reduced the rate of civilian casualties since they spiked in July 2007, continuing tragedies, such as the July 6,

2008 strike on a wedding party and the August 22, 2008 bombing in Azizabad, have greatly undermined local support for the efforts of international forces providing security in Afghanistan.

Civilian Casualties Occur in Emergencies

The 43-page report, "'Troops in Contact': Airstrikes and Civilian Deaths in Afghanistan," analyzes the use of airstrikes by US and NATO forces and resulting civilian casualties, particularly when used to make up for the lack of ground troops and during emergency situations. Human Rights Watch found few civilian deaths resulted from planned airstrikes, while almost all deaths occurred in unplanned airstrikes.

"Rapid response airstrikes have meant higher civilian casualties, while every bomb dropped in populated areas amplifies the chance of a mistake," said Brad Adams, Asia director at Human Rights Watch. "Mistakes by the US and NATO have dramatically decreased public support for the Afghan government and the presence of international forces providing security to Afghans."

The report documents how insurgent forces have contributed to the civilian toll from airstrikes by deploying their forces in populated villages, at times with the specific intent to shield their forces from counterattack, a serious violation of the laws of war. Human Rights Watch found several instances where Taliban forces purposefully used civilians as shields to deter US and NATO attacks.

The Number of Deaths Has Increased Rapidly

In 2006, at least 999 Afghan civilians were killed in fighting related to the armed conflict. Of those, at least 699 died during Taliban attacks (including suicide bombings and other bombings unlawfully targeting civilians) and at least 230 died during US or NATO attacks. Of the latter, 116 were killed by

US or NATO airstrikes. In 2007, at least 1,633 Afghan civilians were killed in fighting related to the armed conflict. Of those, some 950 died during attacks by the various insurgent forces, including the Taliban and al-Qaeda. At least 321 were killed by US or NATO airstrikes. Thus, civilian deaths from US and NATO airstrikes nearly tripled from 2006 to 2007.

In the first seven months of 2008, at least 540 Afghan civilians were killed in fighting related to the armed conflict. Of those, at least 367 died during attacks by the various insurgent forces and 173 died during US or NATO attacks. At least 119 were killed by US or NATO airstrikes. For all periods cited, Human Rights Watch uses the most conservative figures available.

Most cases of civilian deaths from airstrikes occurred during the fluid, rapid-response strikes mostly carried out in support of . . . ground troops who are under insurgent attack.

Human Rights Watch criticized the poor response by US officials when civilian deaths occur. Prior to conducting investigations into airstrikes causing civilian loss, US officials often immediately deny responsibility for civilian deaths or place all blame on the Taliban. US investigations conducted have been unilateral, ponderous, and lacking in transparency, undercutting rather than improving relations with local populations and the Afghan government. A faulty condolence payment system has not provided timely and adequate compensation to assist civilians harmed by US actions.

"The US needs to end the mistakes that are killing so many civilians," said Adams. "The US must also take responsibility, including by providing timely compensation, when its airstrikes kill Afghan civilians. While Taliban shielding is a factor in some civilian deaths, the US shouldn't use this as an excuse when it could have taken better precautions. It is, after all, its bombs that are doing the killing."

Anticipatory Self-Defense Is Sometimes a Factor

Human Rights Watch found that few civilians casualties occurred as the result of planned airstrikes on suspected Taliban targets. Instead, most cases of civilian deaths from airstrikes occurred during the fluid, rapid-response strikes mostly carried out in support of "troops in contact"—ground troops who are under insurgent attack. Such unplanned strikes included situations where US special forces units—normally small in number and lightly armed—came under insurgent attack; in US/NATO attacks in pursuit of insurgent forces who had retreated to populated villages; and in air attacks where US "anticipatory self-defense" rules of engagement applied.

In every case ... where airstrikes hit villages, many civilians had to leave the village because of damage to their homes and fear of further strikes.

Broader Impact of Airstrikes

The effects of airstrikes go beyond civilian deaths. For example, an investigation by the Afghan government found that two battles over a three-day period starting April 30, 2007 in Shindand district resulted in the destruction of numerous homes. In every case investigated by Human Rights Watch where airstrikes hit villages, many civilians had to leave the village because of damage to their homes and fear of further strikes. People from neighboring villages also sometimes fled in fear of future strikes on their villages. This has led to large numbers of internally displaced persons.

Changes in Targeting Tactics

To respond to public concern and complaints from President Hamid Karzai, in July 2007 the NATO-led International Security Assistance Force (ISAF) announced several changes in targeting tactics. These changes include employing smaller munitions, delaying attacks where civilians might be harmed, and turning over house-to-house searches to the Afghan National Army. A review of available evidence suggests that the changes had some impact, as there was a significant drop in civilian casualties due to airstrikes in the last half of 2007, even as the overall tonnage of bombs dropped increased.

Human Rights Watch welcomed these changes in targeting, but remained concerned by continuing civilian casualties from airstrikes, particularly as the number of airstrikes has increased dramatically and the number of deaths and injuries has spiked this summer.

Human Rights Watch called for the US and NATO to address the rising civilian death toll from unplanned airstrikes, and to fix continuing problems with field collateral damage estimation and the inconsistent application of their Rules of Engagement.

"The recent airstrikes killing dozens of Afghans make clear that the system is still broken and that civilians continue to pay the ultimate price," said Adams. "Civilian deaths from airstrikes act as a recruiting tool for the Taliban and risk fatally undermining the international effort to provide basic security to the people of Afghanistan."

5

U.S. Casualties in Iraq Are Not Comparable to Those in Vietnam

Tim Kane and David D. Gentilli

Tim Kane, Ph.D., is Director of the Center for International Trade and Economics; David D. Gentilli is a Research Assistant at The Heritage Foundation.

As American troops continue to fight and die in the global war on terror, some are comparing Iraq to Vietnam. Deployment and casualty numbers, however, show that there are more differences than similarities between the two conflicts. Rather than making misleading comparisons, Americans should be proud of their military, and acknowledge with respect the sacrifice of troops who have lost their lives.

As the global war on terrorism enters its fifth year and American troops continue to fight and die abroad, there is a growing tendency to frame the discussion about troop deployments in the context of wars past, particularly the Vietnam conflict (1965–1973). Such comparisons, while natural, are more likely than not to produce flawed analysis. Each war is unique, and any comparison to other wars invariably suffers from oversimplification. With respect to troop deployments and casualties, comparing the Iraq War with the Vietnam conflict will demonstrate more differences than similarities.

Simply put, there are far fewer U.S. troops in Iraq today than there were in Vietnam in the late 1960s, and there are far

Tim Kane and David D. Gentilli, "Is Iraq Another Vietnam? Not for U.S. Troop Levels," *Heritage Foundation Backgrounder*, July 21, 2006. Copyright © 2006 The Heritage Foundation. Reproduced by permission.

fewer casualties. Second, troop levels are more stable in Iraq. Third, the duration of deployments cannot be compared because U.S. engagement with Iraq has been shorter, and the Iraq conflict is open-ended. Overall, American strategy in Iraq is less reliant on military muscle and more focused on the political and economic aspects of fighting a counter-insurgency. Focusing on political and economic development is the superior strategy, but success will require patience and endurance.

Troop Deployments Then and Now

In Vietnam, the United States employed a flawed strategy referred to as "graduated pressure." The idea behind this was that increasing levels of military force, applied incrementally, could ultimately push the North Vietnamese to some abstract breaking point, achieving victory for the U.S. and South Vietnam. The strategy focused on minimizing costs rather than winning the war, relied on faulty assumptions about the enemy's psychology, and, most of all, offered no real solutions about how to defeat the Communists other than essentially throwing more troops at the problem.

By contrast, U.S. troop levels in Iraq have remained relatively constant for four years. Throughout the conflict, there have been occasional fluctuations in the number of troops, particularly to provide better security for the Iraqi elections, yet annual levels have held steady at roughly 130,000.

During the Vietnam conflict, U.S. troop strength increased dramatically during the first four years, growing by 100,000 extra troops per year and peaking in 1968 at 537,377. In contrast, around the time of the January 2005 Iraqi elections, the number of U.S. troops participating in Operation Iraqi Freedom reached its peak at approximately 159,000. During the third year of the Vietnam conflict (1967), the number of U.S. troops stationed there was 451,752—more than three times the number of troops stationed in Iraq today.

Additionally, America's military is much smaller today than it was during Vietnam. In 1967, the total military force, active and reserve components combined, was just over 3.4 million. Almost 30 percent of the total number of U.S. troops were stationed overseas, compared to 27 percent in 2005—similar percentages of vastly different-sized militaries.

Although the operational tempo as a result of the war on terrorism places great stress on the troops and their families, the numbers show that the current situation is not unusual in a time of war. The strain has been greatest on the National Guard and Reserves, but that is in large part because organizational changes in the Department of Defense that were prompted by the Vietnam conflict place a much greater reliance on the Guard and Reserves today than was the case in Vietnam.

Troop Levels and Casualties

Over 2,500 U.S. service personnel have been killed in Iraq. These deaths are both heroic and tragic, but the total is dwarfed by the number of fatal casualties in the Vietnam conflict, which topped 58,000 by the time the last U.S. troops withdrew. While the war in Iraq certainly presents challenges, the bloodshed has not reached the same level. A report by the U.S. Army's Strategic Studies Institute comparing the Iraq and Vietnam wars concludes that from 1965 to 1973 an average of 134 American military personnel were killed in Vietnam every week. In contrast, the bloodiest month in Iraq saw fewer deaths of U.S. troops when 126 soldiers died in both April and November of 2004. That the average week in Vietnam was deadlier than the worst month in Iraq is a triumph of the force protection efforts of the Pentagon. Yet it is even more a symbol of a significantly smaller engagement.

As a percentage of the total number of troops deployed, the numbers of U.S. soldiers killed in Iraq and Vietnam are comparable. A deployment of 8.7 million U.S. troops in Vietnam, relative to 58,000 fatalities, yields a ratio of seven-tenths of 1 percent. In comparison, the Iraq figures to date are approximately 500,000 deployments and 2,500 fatalities, a ratio of five-tenths of 1 percent.

Over 2,500 U.S. service personnel have been killed in Iraq. These deaths are both heroic and tragic, but the total is dwarfed by the number of fatal casualties in the Vietnam conflict.

What This Means for Americans

Iraq is not Vietnam. The war in Iraq, some 40 years after the Vietnam conflict, is different both quantitatively and qualitatively. In the late 1960s and early 1970s, the ranks of the U.S. military were filled with draftees; now they are filled exclusively with volunteers. In the 1960s, policymakers focused on body counts of the enemy; now they focus on the deaths of our own troops.

Both of these measures miss the point. What should matter to Americans is the mission to secure freedom abroad, because that is why our troops join and serve. However, troop numbers do inform us and dispel some conventional myths.

First, although troop levels have held steady in Iraq for four years, the political winds in Congress have shifted from calling for more troops to calling for fewer troops. It is likely that U.S. troop levels in Iraq will decline as the war enters its fifth year.

Second, by a ratio of nearly 3:1, there are fewer U.S. troops stationed overseas today than there were during the Vietnam conflict, even though the percentage of troops abroad compared to the total force is similar. This shows that the American military's footprint is smaller today, contrary to the myth of a new imperial posture.

Third, Iraq is not a meat grinder, nor is it more deadly than Vietnam. The number of U.S. troop deaths as a proportion of the total number to have served in Iraq is comparable to what it was in Vietnam. Though all wars are dangerous and troops endure many hardships, the argument that Iraq is especially deadly is not supported by the data. The data may, ironically, describe an overemphasis on force protection at the expense of cultural engagement.

Fourth, despite political pressure, the U.S. effort in Iraq places far less emphasis on numbers of troops. Even though there have been mistakes along the way, there has been a greater focus on the political aspect of the counterinsurgency in Iraq than there was in Vietnam.

The most important thing for Americans to remember about the Iraq War is that the vast majority of U.S. military personnel are serving admirably.

Americans Should Be Proud

The most important thing for Americans to remember about the Iraq War is that the vast majority of U.S. military personnel are serving admirably. Sadly, more than 2,500 have been killed, but they have rid the world of a murderous dictatorship that was determined to acquire weapons of mass destruction; they have killed and captured thousands of terrorists; and they have helped a fledgling democracy to beat the odds and secure roots in the Middle East. They have done all this in the face of great adversity and in a restrained manner that should make Americans proud.

6

U.S. Contractors in Iraq Are Hidden Casualties of the War

T. Christian Miller

T. Christian Miller is the author of Blood Money: Wasted Billions, Lost Lives, and Corporate Greed in Iraq. *An award-winning journalist who has worked for the* Los Angeles Times *and the* San Francisco Chronicle, *he is a senior reporter for* ProPublica.

The U.S. military depends on contract workers for many support functions in Iraq and Afghanistan, such as cooking for the troops, laundry, delivery of equipment and supplies, and security. Nearly 1600 of these contract workers, including both Americans and foreign nationals, have died in the two war zones, and thousands more have been injured. Their sacrifice is largely unrecognized and those who survive their injuries do not have access to the veteran's health care system and other networks of support.

R*eporting from Central Point, Ore.*—A nurse rocked him awake as pale dawn light crept into the room. "C'mon now, c'mon," the nurse murmured. "Time to get up."

Reggie Lane was once a hulking man of 260 pounds. Friends called him "Big Dad." Now, he weighed less than 200 pounds and his brain was severely damaged. He groaned angry, wordless cries.

The nurse moved fast. Two bursts of deodorant spray under each useless arm. Then he dressed Lane and used a mechanical arm to hoist him into a wheelchair.

He wheeled Big Dad down a hallway and parked the chair in a beige dining room, in front of a picture window. Outside stretched a green valley of pear trees filled with white blossoms.

Lane's head fell forward, his chin buried in his chest. His legs crossed and uncrossed involuntarily. His left index finger was rigid and pointed, as if frozen in permanent accusation.

He's a human being who fought for his country. He doesn't deserve to be thrown away.

In 2004, Lane was driving a fuel truck in Iraq for a defense contractor when insurgents attacked his convoy with rocket-propelled grenades. For most of the five years since, Lane, now 60, has spent his days in silence—a reminder of the hidden costs of relying on civilian contract workers to support the U.S. war effort.

His wife, Linda, said visiting her husband was difficult. They were childhood friends and fiercely loyal to each other. On this spring morning, she caressed his hand and told him she loved him.

"He was a good man. He paid his bills. He took care of his family," she said, her breathing labored from a pulmonary disease. "He's a human being who fought for his country. He doesn't deserve to be thrown away."

The U.S. Depends on Contract Workers

In Iraq and Afghanistan, the U.S. military has depended on contract workers more than in any previous conflict—to cook meals for troops, wash laundry, deliver supplies and protect diplomats, among other tasks. Tens of thousands of civilians have worked in the two battle zones, often facing the same dangers as U.S. troops and suffering the same kinds of injuries.

Contract workers from the U.S. have been mostly men, primarily middle-aged, many of them military veterans drawn by money, patriotism or both, according to interviews and public records. They are police officers, truck drivers, firefighters, mechanics and craftsmen, mostly from rural corners of America, especially the South.

Nearly 1,600 civilian workers—both Americans and foreign nationals—have died in the two war zones. Thousands more have been injured. (More than 5,200 U.S. service members have been killed and 35,000 wounded.)

Many of the civilians have come home as military veterans in all but name, sometimes with lifelong disabilities but without the support network available to returning troops.

There are no veterans' halls for civilian workers, no Gold Star Wives, no military hospitals. Politicians pay little attention to their problems, and the military has not publicized their contributions.

"These guys are like the Vietnam vets of this generation," said Lee Frederiksen, a psychologist who worked for Mission Critical Psychological Services, a Chicago-based firm that provides counseling for war zone workers. "The normal support that you would get if you were injured in the line of duty as a police officer or if you were injured in the military . . . just doesn't exist."

Many of the civilians have come home as military veterans in all but name, sometimes with lifelong disabilities but without the support network available to returning troops.

Contract Workers Do Not Receive the Same Support

Herbert J. Lanese, former chief executive of DynCorp International, one of the largest employers of civilian workers in Iraq and Afghanistan, said: "These are people who have given their lives in the service of our country. They are the unappreciated patriots of our country at this point in time."

Lane was born in Ventura and moved to Grants Pass, Ore., when he turned 12. He met Linda there, and the two grew up together.

After high school, Reggie enlisted in the Army and went to Vietnam. He and Linda found each other after he returned. By then, each had been married and divorced, and each had a child.

These are people who have given their lives in the service of our country. They are the unappreciated patriots of our country at this point in time.

As a pair, they were inseparable. Reggie was steady, strong. Linda was energetic and outgoing. They eventually found work as a truck-driving team, steering tractor-trailers across the country.

His CB radio handle was "Grizzly." Hers was "Wild Cat." He loved country music and Tom Clancy novels, G. Gordon Liddy's talk show and Honda motorcycles. She loved the open road, the speed of the truck.

"We went to see the big wide world driving a truck. What an adventure," Linda recalled.

But work was haphazard, and the pay was modest. Together, they made about $32,000 a year. They had a hard time keeping up with bills and twice filed for bankruptcy.

In the late 1990s, they sold their home in Oregon and moved to Montana, where land was cheaper.

In the fall of 2003, Linda heard that defense contractor KBR Inc. was hiring truck drivers to deliver fuel, food and supplies for the military in Iraq. The salary was $88,000 a year, more than they had ever earned.

"We wouldn't be on easy street," Linda said. "But we wouldn't be stressed."

By November, Reggie was on his way to Iraq. He arrived during a turbulent period, with the insurgency raging. Convoys regularly came under attack. The trucks were not armored.

"He didn't go over there to fight a war. He went over there because [KBR] said, 'You'll have armed guards,'" Linda said. "They promised big money. 'You'll be protected, no problem.'"

On April 9, 2004, Reggie Lane and a friend, Jason Hurd, rolled out of a base south of Baghdad to deliver fuel to Balad, north of the city. The convoy was outside Baghdad when gunfire rang out. Hurd saw Reggie's truck careen to the side of the road.

Hurd pulled over. A rocket-propelled grenade had shattered the windshield. Reggie was lying face-up on the shoulder of the road. His right arm was gone below the elbow. His face was covered in shrapnel wounds. He was drenched in blood.

The rest of the convoy moved ahead, apparently oblivious. Hurd fumbled with Reggie's arm, trying to apply a tourniquet. Then a group of military vehicles pulled over to help.

He Was Hit by a Rocket-Propelled Grenade

Soldiers helped stabilize Lane, who shuddered awake and asked for water. An Army helicopter evacuated him to a U.S. base, where he was put on an emergency flight to Germany.

Linda got the news from a military doctor. A few days later, Reggie called. He told her not to worry.

"I still got one arm left to hug you with," he said.

It was the last conversation she would have with her husband.

Two days later, another military doctor in Germany called Linda, asking permission to perform an emergency tracheotomy on Reggie. A blood clot had dislodged, blocking the flow of blood to his brain.

"My head is spinning. I'm trying to digest what they're telling me," Linda said. "I'm deciding this long-distance by phone, and it's someone I love."

Ten days after the attack, Reggie Lane was on a flight back to the U.S., headed to a Houston hospital. KBR paid to have Linda meet her husband in Texas.

She was unprepared for the sight. A raw, red stump was all that remained of his right arm. There was a hole in his throat. She could see his intestines, which were left exposed to aid in cleaning out shrapnel. His body was swollen and purple. He was unresponsive, his pupils mere pinpoints.

Over the next nine months, Linda lived out of a hotel in downtown Houston. She became her husband's advocate, navigating a complex medical world with little guidance.

"It was a lot of one foot in front of the other. I was pretty devastated," she said.

Slowly, Lane's condition improved. Toward the end of his hospital stay, he could respond to questions. He would say: "Love Linda." He was trying to stand up with help.

"By the time he left, he was interacting, communicating," said Dr. Sunil Kothari, a neurosurgeon who coordinated Reggie's care at the Institute for Rehabilitation and Research (TIRR) Memorial Hermann in Houston, one of the country's top rehabilitation hospitals for brain injury. "Near the end, he was beginning to answer questions, starting to vocalize."

In January 2005, doctors cleared Reggie for release. He was going home.

Nursing Care Was Inadequate

Grants Pass had a handful of nursing homes. They provided physical and speech therapy, but Linda was dissatisfied with the care. She confronted workers at one home, leading to Reggie's discharge. He returned to a hospital.

Linda was dealing with her own health problems. Her weight ballooned. She was admitted to the hospital repeatedly with breathing difficulties.

As Linda searched for a home for her husband, she got into a dispute with American International Group Inc. [AIG], the insurance carrier for KBR. Linda wanted her husband close to home. She said AIG insisted that he go to a facility in Portland, where care was less expensive than in the hospital.

Troops injured in Iraq are guaranteed care at Veterans Affairs facilities. In contrast, contract workers depend on workers' compensation insurance paid for by the federal government under the Defense Base Act. They often must fight with insurers to get medical bills paid.

Linda hired a lawyer, and AIG relented, allowing Reggie to be placed in an adult foster care home near Grants Pass.

Troops injured in Iraq are guaranteed care at Veterans Affairs facilities. In contrast, contract workers . . . often must fight with insurers to get medical bills paid.

The lawyer, Roger Hawkins of Los Angeles, said it was the least Reggie deserved.

"You look in his eyes and you see that somewhere, he realizes what is going on," Hawkins said. "He's sitting there with his arm missing and knowing that he's never going to get better."

AIG and KBR declined to comment on the case.

Reggie's mental state had gradually declined since he'd left Houston. Before, he spoke. Now he descended into long silences broken only by grunts.

He Needed More Stimulation

Told of Lane's condition, Kothari, who treated him in Houston, expressed concern.

"Decline is not typical," Kothari said. "If someone goes to a nursing facility, if they happen not to get stimuli, it means the brain could not heal as well as it would otherwise."

Jim Gregg, operator of the foster care home where Lane was placed, said the facility was not equipped for advanced physical or speech therapy. In their home on a 4-acre farm, Gregg and his wife provided basic medical care and monitoring to half a dozen elderly patients.

"It's a boring life. He just sits here," Gregg said. "It's not a stimulating environment."

Gregg closed his facility earlier this year, and Lane was moved to another foster home. The total cost of Lane's care for the rest of his life could be as much as $8.9 million, according to an AIG estimate. The bill will be paid by the federal government, which reimburses insurers for combat-related claims from war zone workers.

Linda Lane died July 10. She had been hospitalized after suffering respiratory distress, family members said.

Reggie let out a wail when relatives told him the news. "I had never heard anything like that before," said Bev Glasgow, who runs Lane's current foster home.

Glasgow arranged for a van to take Reggie to a memorial service for his wife. It was held in a state park alongside the Rogue River. Under the shade of scrub oak and aspen, he watched as Linda's family and friends sang "Amazing Grace" and looked at old photos of the couple.

Diane Firestone, Reggie's sister, visited him shortly after Linda's death. She said the family accepted that Reggie's condition was unlikely to change. But, she said, they did not believe his sacrifices had been adequately recognized, by his company or the country.

She knelt beside her brother and asked him about the attack on his convoy.

"Hey, Reg," she said. "Do you know it's been five years? It doesn't seem that long to me. Does it seem that long to you?"

Reggie blinked twice, hard—his signal for yes.

7

Iraqi Military Interpreters Must Fight for Compensation for Injuries

Dubai News.Net

Dubai News.Net is owned by Mainstream Media EC, which is incorporated in Bahrain by Australian owners.

Iraqis who served the U.S. government as interpreters following the invasion of Iraq in 2003 risked their lives to provide a service that was critical to the U.S. mission. U.S. law requires that military contractors injured while performing their services be covered with health and disability insurance, but most are not receiving the care they need. The insurance company that covers interpreters—American International Group (AIG)—requires those filing claims to provide proof, such as police records, to document that their injuries were received in connection with their work. Unable to produce the required paperwork, many Iraqi interpreters injured while performing their jobs have ended up destitute, and have not received medical care for their wounds.

Following the Iraq invasion the Pentagon, through a private contractor, employed around 8,000 Iraqi interpreters.

Risking being targeted as collaborators, the interpreters assisted U.S. forces on the ground in major offensives, traveled with convoys, and got caught up in other vulnerable situations.

Nearly 400 have been killed in the intervening years, and over 1,200 injured.

According to a *Los Angeles Times* report, which followed an investigation by the newspaper in conjunction with *ProPublica,* scores of interpreters assisting U.S. forces in Afghanistan have also been killed or wounded.

An insurance program funded by American taxpayers was supposed to provide a safety net for interpreters and their families in the event of injury or death, the *LA Times* reported. Yet for many, the benefits have fallen painfully short of what was promised.

The media groups' investigation revealed that insurers have delayed or denied claims for disability payments and death benefits, citing a lack of police reports or other documentary evidence that interpreters' injuries or deaths were related to their work for the military. Critics, says the *Times* report, including some U.S. Army officers, say it is absurd to expect Iraqis and Afghans to be able to document the cause of injuries suffered in a war zone.

Iraqi interpreters taken to neighboring Jordan for medical treatment told the investigation team they were pressured to accept lump-sum settlements from insurers, rather than a stream of lifetime benefits potentially worth more, and were told that if they didn't sign, they would be sent back home, a potential death sentence for Iraqis associated with the American war effort.

Interpreters who have immigrated to the United States as refugees have ended up penniless, on food stamps or in menial jobs because their benefits under the U.S. insurance program are based on wages and living costs in their home countries, the *LA Times* report said. Payments intended to provide a decent standard of living in Iraq or Afghanistan leave the recipients below the poverty level in the United States.

An insurance program ... was supposed to provide a safety net for interpreters and their families ... Yet for many, the benefits have fallen painfully short of what was promised.

Iraqi Malek Hadi was working with U.S. MP [military police]s outside Baghdad when a homemade explosive detonated beneath his Humvee in September 2006. The blast tore off his right leg, mangled the left and sheared off several fingers.

Today, Hadi, 25, lives alone in a crime-ridden neighborhood in Arlington, Texas. He struggles to climb the stairs to his second-floor apartment on crutches, says the *Los Angeles Times*. He has been diagnosed with post-traumatic stress disorder but is not receiving treatment because his insurer has refused to pay for it.

He lives on $612 a month in disability payments, the maximum available under the war-zone insurance system.

"When we were in Iraq, we were exactly like the soldiers," Hadi said. "Why are we treated differently now?"

Interpreters Are Crucial to the Mission

Retired U.S. Army Col. Joel Armstrong, who served in Iraq and was a leading proponent of the 2007 troop buildup, or "surge," that helped reduce violence in the country, said Iraqi interpreters were crucial to the strategy's success.

"Without them, you really can't operate effectively as a force. It's just impossible," Armstrong told the *Los Angeles Times*. "It is deplorable, he added, that interpreters injured while assisting American troops have had to fight for benefits."

"Every American should feel terrible about it," he said. "It's a shame."

American International Group Inc., or AIG, the principal provider of insurance coverage for interpreters in Iraq, declined to answer detailed questions on its policies or comment on specific cases.

Marie Ali, a spokeswoman for the AIG unit that sold the coverage, said the company "is committed to handling every claim professionally, ethically and fairly. In all cases, it is our policy to respect the privacy of our customers and claimants and not discuss the specifics of individual claims."

Under a World War II-era law known as the Defense Base Act, companies working under contract for the U.S. military overseas must provide workers' compensation insurance for their employees, both Americans and foreign nationals. The cost of the coverage is built into Pentagon contracts and so is ultimately paid by taxpayers, said the *Los Angeles Times* report.

8

Media Coverage of Returning Fallen Soldiers Is To Be Allowed Again

Editor & Publisher

Editor & Publisher *is considered an authoritative journal covering all aspects of the North American newspaper industry.*

News coverage of the return of fallen soldiers, including photographs of flag-covered caskets, has been permitted since the Obama administration reversed an 18-year-old ban on media presence at ceremonies for the soldiers. The services are held at Dover Air Force Base in Delaware. Response to the change in policy, however, has been mixed. While some families do not want the media to be present, the majority believe that attending the return of the caskets is a way of showing respect. Under the new policy, media can attend and contact the family only if the family agrees.

In the weeks since the Pentagon ended an 18-year ban on media coverage of fallen soldiers returning to the U.S., most families given the option have allowed reporters and photographers to witness the solemn ceremonies that mark the arrival of flag-draped transfer cases.

Critics had warned that military families needed privacy and peace activists might exploit the images, but so far the coverage has not caused problems.

"Remember That Excuse for Not Showing Coffins Coming Home from War? Turns Out Families OK With It," *Editor & Publisher*, April 27, 2009. Copyright © 2009 Nielsen Business Media, Inc. Reproduced by permission.

Air Force Staff Sgt. Phillip A. Myers of Hopewell, Va., who died April 4 in Afghanistan, was the first combat casualty whose return to American soil was witnessed by the media. He was to be buried with full military honors Monday afternoon at Arlington National Cemetery.

With permission from his widow, Aimee, the military opened Dover Air Force Base earlier this month so reporters and photographers could chronicle his return. The mortuary there is the entry point for service members killed overseas.

The ban on media coverage dated back to 1991, when President George H.W. Bush imposed it during the Persian Gulf War. It was cast as a way to protect the privacy of grieving families, but critics argued that officials were trying to hide the human and political cost of war.

"I think it was to protect the government's butt," said David Pautsch, who allowed the media to witness the return of his son Jason, an Army corporal from Davenport, Iowa, who was killed with four other soldiers in a bombing in Iraq.

Since the ban was lifted, 19 families have been asked whether they wanted media coverage of their loved one's return and 14 have said yes.

He said the ban was more about minimizing the political impact of Americans dying overseas.

"I think it was a reaction against the second-guessing of our country's mission," he said.

Since the ban was lifted, 19 families have been asked whether they wanted media coverage of their loved one's return and 14 have said yes.

"That's a pretty good majority," Lt. Col. Les Melnyk, a Pentagon spokesman, said earlier this month, when 16 families had been asked and 13 had consented. He said, though, that it's still too early to tell whether military families favor the new policy.

Rose Alexander, a spokeswoman for the Air Force Mortuary Affairs Office, said reporters have been cooperative and there haven't been any problems.

Even if no one from the media shows up, the Department of Defense films each casualty arrival for which consent is given and presents a recording to the family.

Media interest has fallen off sharply since almost 40 reporters, photographers and camera operators turned out to document the arrival of Myers' body. At a more recent casualty arrivals, the only media representative was a lone photographer from The Associated Press.

Even if no one from the media shows up, the Department of Defense films each casualty arrival for which consent is given and presents a recording to the family.

Christie Woods initially declined media coverage of the return of her husband, Staff Sgt. Gary L. Woods Jr., of Lebanon Junction, Ky., who was killed along with Jason Pautsch. She changed her mind so family members who couldn't travel to Dover would have the video, according to casualty assistance officer Sgt. Joseph Chapman.

Families must make the difficult decision about whether to allow media coverage, and whether to travel to Dover, within hours of being told of a loved one's death.

The military's long-term goal is to have each service member make the decision before deploying to a combat zone rather than having the family choose after the fact.

While survivors are asked whether they consent to media coverage and want to travel to Dover, a policy memo issued by Defense Secretary Robert Gates states that media contact with family members will be allowed "only if specifically requested" by the family.

Mortuary affairs office officials say they will help facilitate a meeting if a family indicates that it would like to talk with the media. So far, the Pautsch family has been the only one to do so. David Pautsch said he understands the military is trying to be sensitive but believes families should be asked whether they want to speak to the media rather than having to volunteer their desire.

"We shouldn't be afraid of letting people express their opinions," he said.

9

Media Coverage of Fallen Soldiers Is Not Transparent Enough

Kevin Baron

Kevin Baron is the Washington bureau reporter for Stars and Stripes, *covering the Pentagon, national security, military and foreign affairs.*

As a result of recent changes in Pentagon policy, families of fallen soldiers can choose to ban the media from covering their family member's return, or to permit only military cameras to be present. However, some feel this decision should not be left to families because coverage of the ceremonies at Dover informs the public of the real costs of the war, and is a way of keeping public officials responsible to the public for the decisions they make.

The Pentagon has amended its policy regarding media coverage of the flag-draped coffins of dead U.S. service members returning to Dover AFB [Air Force Base]. Families now have the power to permit military cameras to record the event and ban independent news media from doing the same.

But why?

The base policy remains: families are asked by military officials before the U.S. arrival of their deceased relative if they will allow media coverage of the "dignified transfer" (Don't call it a ceremony.) of "transfer cases" (Don't call them coffins.)

arriving from the Overseas Contingency Operation (Don't call it the war in Afghanistan.)

Previously, if the family said "no"—nothing was recorded by anyone. If they said "yes", the event was recorded by independent media, usually a single AP [Associated Press] photographer, as well as Defense Department video and still cameras.

Families Can Ban the Media

Now, families can ask for Pentagon photographers, but reject the media presence, effectively banning the public from seeing images of the event until a later time, which seems a reversion against the Pentagon's pledge of greater media transparency.

There is background madness to this method. When the Pentagon of the previous Bush administration banned news photographers and reporters from Dover AFB from covering the return of dead American bodies from war, the department said their policy was to protect military families from____.

Families can ask for Pentagon photographers, but reject the media presence, effectively banning the public from seeing images of the event until a later time.

You can fill-in-the-blank with whatever Pentagon spin you want. They didn't want the American public to see 4,000+ coffins offloaded from cargo planes between 2001 and 2009—and you didn't.

(Actually the ban dates to the 1990s after the U.S. invasion of Panama, when a network nightly news program broadcast a split screen image of returning flag-draped coffins on one half and President George H. W. Bush laughing at a separate event on the other half. So much for media coverage at Dover.)

Media newsrooms and public watchdogs protested that the public deserved a record of the war in its entirety, especially back in 2001 and 2003, when the idea and imagery of America at war was so impactful.

The line went: if the Pentagon was going to allow news crews to record the happily cheering families running across tarmacs to greet their returning heroes, journalists must also be allowed to document those who come home from the most controversial war since Vietnam in boxes—the practical impact of policy decisions.

The Pentagon said such a record did exist: their own defense department media crews recorded the Dover returns and families could get copies. Some family members simply could not make the last-minute trip to Delaware to meet their loved ones' remains.

One problem: the U.S. public—including news organizations—could request to see those supposedly private pictures and recordings per the Freedom of Information Act. That's how several photos of military coffins—er, "transfer cases"—were published in the early years of the Iraq war.

Hundreds Came Back in the Dark

So the Pentagon stopped its internal recording entirely. As a result, hundreds of fallen warriors and victims of the longest war in U.S. history came home in the dark.

This year [2009], Defense Secretary Robert Gates reversed the total ban, but approved a complex set of rules.

A *Washington Post* article last week discovered that the policy had been changed. Now, families can once again choose to have only the Pentagon record the event, but ban the media.

I doubt many news organizations will submit FOIA [Freedom of Information Act] requests for those images. Few news organizations attend Dover arrivals. The base is a good 2–3 hour drive from Washington, D.C. Nobody maintains camera crews there. When a spectacular event occurs—like the stress clinic shooting where 5 troops were murdered—more show up (22 separate news organizations for that one, including Stars and Stripes). The AP is the only news organization recording each return they are permitted—as hometown papers usually want to publish the image.

And its unclear if the base and the Pentagon would honor timely media requests for images of arrival ceremonies the press was shut out from. How long will it take? The FOIA process is not known for its expediency. One defense writer last week told me he just received a pile of Defense Department documents that he had requested several years ago.

But here's a new fact to go with the new policy: in the past six months, 15 percent of all families have chosen the option of DoD [Department of Defense]-only recording, the Post reported. Along with the 60 percent already allowing media on the tarmac, that means fully 75 percent of the families who were asked if they wanted SOME publicly available recording of their loved one's return have said YES.

For Secretary Gates, the question of media coverage has always been about the family's wishes.

For others, even if 100 percent of the familes agreed to media coverage, the choice should not be left to them. War is a decision made by elected officials and servants beholden to the public, including military service members. The record of war, they say, also belongs to the public.

Fully 75 percent of the families who were asked if they wanted SOME publicly available recording of their loved one's return have said YES.

UPDATE: Pentagon spokesman Bryan Whitman said . . . that the issue of FOIA had come up early in the deliberations over rules on Dover media coverage, which they had wanted to remain "family centric". So why the change? The department wanted to give families who could not make the trip to Dover an option to have a video copy, he said.

"We've always offered a video to family members if they've requested it from a government camera out at Dover," he said.

Families of the dead are informed that if they choose that government-recorded option only, the imagery and video is still available to the public via FOIA, Whitman said. He pushed back at the notion that 75 percent of families have said "yes" to coverage, when just 57.5 percent have accepted full media coverage.

"They believe—you have to kind of put yourself in their shoes—they believe that all they're getting is a tape of the situation. Their expectation is that it will never be shown," Whitman said, because the media already has plenty of Dover images to tell their story.

"Nobody's going to FOIA that stuff," he said. "The media have access to what they want, the families have what they want, if they can't make it."

10

Media Interest in Covering the Return of Fallen Soldiers Has Fallen

Matt Towery

Matt Towery is the author of Paranoid Nation: The Real Story of the 2009 Fight for the Presidency; *he heads the polling and political information firm InsiderAdvantage.*

In 2009 the Obama administration reversed a ban on media coverage of the flag-draped caskets of American soldiers. However, since the policy change, media interest has waned. Towery compares the media coverage of the events following the death of Michael Jackson to that given to those who have given their lives in defense of their country, and suggests that the true heroes do not get the coverage that they deserve.

I'm not a Michael Jackson hater. I liked his music, partly because it was part of my life as a young man. And I never judge people and their morals. Unless convicted by a court of law, it's really between them, the truth—whatever that might be—and their maker.

But as thousands of people filled a huge arena in Los Angeles this week, and millions more were glued to their television sets; as accolades unlimited were spoken about the late "King of Pop," my mind was on how seven other Americans might be honored. You see, on July 6, seven American troops were killed in Afghanistan, making it the deadliest day for our military there in nearly a year.

Their bodies would no doubt be shipped back to our nation in those standard military coffins. The American flags draping these simple containers would be the sole hope for added color, grandeur, or beauty. The coffins would have no stately gold or magnificent silk to hold their precious remains.

It is likely that no lottery will be necessary to gain tickets to their respective funerals or memorial services. No one will offer up a thin dime on eBay or Craigslist to have the honor of being present when the soldiers' families and friends gather to remember their fallen loved ones. I doubt many celebrities will be present at any of these somber occasions. Rev. Al Sharpton will have moved on to his next gig.

Their bodies would no doubt be shipped back to our nation in those standard military coffins. The American flags draping these simple containers would be the sole hope for added color, grandeur, or beauty.

I feel certain we will not see repeated special TV broadcasts about the acts of bravery and heroism these soldiers performed as they fought to keep our nation from having to again encounter firsthand an organization active in Afghanistan and Pakistan that would, if given the chance, act to topple another American building. *Entertainment Tonight* won't cover these deaths because, hey, they aren't entertaining.

I guess you get the picture.

I'm not here to put down those who were touched by and who grieved over the death of Jackson. It would be just as easy to name-call and dwell on Jackson's bad past experiences as it would be to remember his immense talent and the songs that were so much a part of my life as I was growing up.

What is tougher is to describe the lives of these seven brave Americans who were blown up—murdered—in a rough, cruel, terrible foreign land. We don't know anything about them. But in another way we do. We know what they symbolize.

They symbolize the very best of our nation. They symbolize honor, bravery and sacrifice. They represent greatness. They represent security for my family and me, and for yours and you.

For all we know, a few of the soldiers might have had rough patches in their own personal lives. Perhaps not. But just as we could be thrilled watching Michael Jackson doing his famed "Moonwalk," we sure as hell could take time out to notice these brave men and women who are doing what most of us never have or never would: fight and die for this country.

No, there will likely be no JumboTrons at the final services for these fallen soldiers. The last music that their loving families and friends will hear will be the simple melody of "Taps."

I am but one of hundreds of nationally syndicated columnists. In getting noticed by me there is no cachet of a Barbara Walters or a network anchor to imprint on the brief biographies of the fallen soldiers. But I can try to do them justice. So here, with my "ticket" in hand, I will mount my own platform and speak for the many who I know would join me.

Thank you to the fallen warriors. Thank you for dying for me and for every other American. Thank you to your families who knew you were in harm's way, performing heroic tasks that really mean something. Tasks that might decide in years to come whether passengers on some airplane, or workers in some high rise will live or die.

No, there will likely be no JumboTrons at the final services for these fallen soldiers. The last music that their loving families and friends will hear will be the simple melody of "Taps."

And then the heroes' closest relatives will be handed that beautiful flag. It won't equal the gold and flowers for a king. But it will be all this nation can offer to heroes. If you ask me, I'd rather have the flag.

11

The Costs of Caring for U.S. War Casualties Are Enormous

Andrew Stephen

Andrew Stephen was appointed U.S. editor of the New States-man *in 2001, having been its Washington correspondent and weekly columnist since 1998.*

Wars in Iraq and Afghanistan have resulted in large numbers of soldiers being wounded in action. Serious injuries, including limb amputations and head injuries, have left thousands of soldiers physically disabled while others suffer from post-traumatic stress disorder. The costs of providing medical care and disability compensation to those who have been seriously injured in Iraq and Afghanistan could be as high as $2.5 trillion.

America won't simply be paying with its dead. The Pentagon is trying to silence economists who predict that several decades of care for the wounded will amount to an unbelievable $2.5 trillion.

They roar in every day, usually direct from the Landstuhl US air-force base in the Rhineland: giant C-17 cargo planes capable of lifting and flying the 65-tonne M1 Abrams tank to battlefields anywhere in the world. But Landstuhl is the first staging post for transporting most of the American wounded in Iraq and Afghanistan back to the United States, and these planes act as CCATs ("critical care air transport") with their AETs—"aeromedical evacuation teams" of doctors, nurses and medical technicians, whose task is to make sure that gravely wounded US troops arrive alive and fit enough for intensive treatment at the Walter Reed Army Medical Centre, just six miles up the road from me in Washington.

These days it is de rigueur for all politicians, ranging from President Bush and Ibrahim al-Jaafari (Iraq's "prime minister") to junior congressmen, to visit the 113-acre Walter Reed complex to pay tribute to the valour of horribly wounded soldiers. Last Christmas, the centre was so overwhelmed by the 500,000 cards and presents it received for wounded soldiers that it announced it could accept no more.

... we have discovered that the administration has been putting out two entirely separate and conflicting sets of numbers of those wounded in the wars.

Yet the story of the US wounded reveals yet another deception by the Bush administration, masking monumental miscalculations that will haunt generations to come. Thanks to the work of a Harvard professor and former Clinton administration economist named Linda Bilmes, and some other hard-working academics, we have discovered that the administration has been putting out two entirely separate and conflicting sets of numbers of those wounded in the wars.

This might sound like chicanery by George W Bush and his cronies—or characteristic incompetence—but Bilmes and Professor Joseph Stiglitz, the Nobel laureate economist from Columbia University, have established not only that the number wounded in Iraq and Afghanistan is far higher than the Pentagon has been saying, but that looking after them alone could cost present and future US taxpayers a sum they estimate to be $536bn, but which could get considerably bigger still. Just one soldier out of the 1.4 million troops so far deployed who has returned with a debilitating brain injury, for example, may need round-the-clock care for five, six, or even seven decades. In present-day money, according to one study, care for that soldier alone will cost a minimum of $4.3m.

However, let us first backtrack to 2002–2003 to try to establish why the administration's sums were so wildly off-target. Documents just obtained under the Freedom of Information Act show how completely lost the Bush administration was in Neverland when it came to Iraq: Centcom, the main top-secret military planning unit at Donald Rumsfeld's Pentagon, predicted in its war plan that only 5,000 US troops would be required in Iraq by the end of 2006.

Rummy's deputy Paul Wolfowitz was such a whizz at the economics of it all that he confidently told us that Iraq would "really finance its own reconstruction". Rumsfeld himself reported that the administration had come up with "a number that's something under $50bn" as the cost of the war. Larry Lindsey, then assistant to the president on economic policy at the White House, warned that it might actually soar to as much as $200bn—with the result that Bush did as he habitually does with those who do not produce convenient facts and figures to back up his fantasies: he sacked him.

Estimating long-term costs using even the second, moderate scenario, Bilmes tells me: "I think we are now approaching a figure of $2.5 trillion."

From official statistics supplied by the non-partisan Congressional Budget Office, we now know that the Iraq war is costing roughly $200m a day, or $6bn every month; the total bill so far is $400bn. But, in their studies, Bilmes and Stiglitz consider three scenarios that were not even conceivable to Bush, Rummy, Wolfowitz *et al* back in 2003. In the first, incurring the lowest future costs, troops will start to be withdrawn this year and be out by 2010. The second assumes that there will be a gradual withdrawal that will be complete by

2015. The third envisages the participation of two million servicemen and women, with the war going on past 2016.

Estimating long-term costs using even the second, moderate scenario, Bilmes tells me: "I think we are now approaching a figure of $2.5 *trillion*." This, she says, "includes three kinds of costs. It includes the cash costs of running the combat operations, the long-term costs of replenishing military equipment and taking care of the veterans, and [increased costs] at the Pentagon. And then it includes the economic cost, which is the differential between reservists' pay in their civilian jobs and what they're paid in the military—and the macroeconomic costs, such as the percentage of the oil-price increase."

Let me pause to explain those deceptive figures. Look at the latest official toll of US fatalities and wounded in the media, and you will see something like 3,160 dead and 23,785 wounded (that "includes 13,250 personnel who returned to duty within 72 hours", the *Washington Post* told us helpfully on 4 March). From this, you might assume that only 11,000 or so troops, in effect, have been wounded in Iraq. But Bilmes discovered that the Bush administration was keeping two separate sets of statistics of those wounded: one (like the above) issued by the Pentagon and therefore used by the media, and the other by the Department of Veterans Affairs—a government department autonomous from the Pentagon. At the beginning of this year, the Pentagon was putting out a figure of roughly 23,000 wounded, but the VA was quietly saying that more than 50,000 had, in fact, been wounded.

Casualty Conspiracy

To draw attention to her academic findings, Bilmes wrote a piece for the *Los Angeles Times* of 5 January 2007 in which she quoted the figure of "more than 50,000 wounded Iraq war soldiers". The reaction from the Pentagon was fury. An assistant secretary there named Dr William Winkenwerder phoned her personally to complain. Bilmes recalls: "He said, 'Where did you get those numbers from?'" She explained to Winkenwerder that the 50,000 figure came from the VA, and faxed him copies of official US government documents that proved her point. Winkenwerder backed down.

Matters did not rest there. Despite its independence from the Pentagon, the VA is run by Robert James Nicholson, a former Republican Party chairman and Bush's loyal political appointee. Following Bilmes's exchange with Winkenwerder—on 10 January, to be precise—the number of wounded listed on the VA website dropped from 50,508 to 21,649. The Bush administration had, once again, turned reality on its head to concur with its claims. "The whole thing is scary," Bilmes says. "I have never been conspiracy-minded, but watching them change the numbers on the website—it's extraordinary."

What Bilmes had discovered was that the tally of US fatalities in Iraq and Afghanistan included the outcome of "non-hostile actions", most commonly vehicle accidents. But the Pentagon's statistics of the *wounded* did not. Even troops incapacitated for life in Iraq or Afghanistan—but not in "hostile situations"—were not being counted, although they will require exactly the same kind of medical care back home as soldiers similarly wounded in battle. Bilmes and Stiglitz had set out, meantime, to explore the ratio of wounded to deaths in previous American wars. They found that in the First World War, on average 1.8 were wounded for every fatality; in the Second World War, 1.6; in Korea, 2.8; in Vietnam, 2.6; and, in the first Gulf war in 1991, 1.2. In this war, 21st-century medical care and better armour have inflated the numbers of the wounded-but-living, leading Bilmes to an astounding conclusion: for every soldier dying in Iraq or Afghanistan today, *16* are being wounded. The Pentagon insists the figure is nearer nine—but, either way, the economic implications for the future are phenomenal.

So far, more than 200,000 veterans from the current Iraq or Afghanistan wars have been treated at VA centres. Twenty per cent of those brought home are suffering from serious brain or spinal injuries, or the severing of more than one limb, and a further 20 per cent from amputations, blindness or deafness, severe burns, or other dire conditions. "Every person injured on active duty is going to be a long-term cost of the war," says Bilmes. If we compare the financial ramifications of the first Gulf war to the present one, the implications become even more stark. Despite its brevity, even the 1991 Gulf war exacted a heavy toll: 48.4 per cent of veterans sought medical care, and 44 per cent filed disability claims. Eighty-eight per cent of these claims were granted, meaning that 611,729 veterans from the first Gulf war are now receiving disability benefits; a large proportion are suffering from psychiatric illnesses, including post-traumatic stress disorder and depression.

More than a third of those returning from the current wars, too, have already been diagnosed as suffering from similar conditions. But although the VA has 207 walk-in "vet centres" and other clinics and offices throughout the US, it is a bureaucracy under siege. It has a well-deserved reputation for providing excellent healthcare for America's 24 million veterans, but is quite unable to cope with a workload that the Bush administration did not foresee.

What Bilmes had discovered was that the tally of US fatalities in Iraq and Afghanistan included the outcome of "non-hostile actions", most commonly vehicle accidents. But the Pentagon's statistics of the wounded did not.

The Unknown Unknowns

There is now a backlog of 400,000 claims from veterans and waiting lists of months, some of which "render . . . care virtually inaccessible", in the words of Frances Murphy, the VA's own deputy under-secretary for health. Claims are expected to hit 874,000 this year, 930,000 in 2008. Casualties returning from Iraq meanwhile outnumber other patients at Walter Reed 17 to one, and many have to be put up at nearby hotels and motels rather than in the hospital beds they desperately need. Suicide attempts are frequent; often the less wounded end up having to care for the more seriously wounded.

Since I researched this piece, the *Washington Post* has published a series of articles outlining the chaos at Walter Reed and elsewhere. Undercover reporters found soldiers suffering from schizophrenia, post-traumatic stress and other brain injuries, occupying rooms infested with mice and cockroaches. The ensuing furore resulted in the sacking of the general in charge. Even Bush says he is "deeply troubled" by these "unacceptable" conditions at Walter Reed, but his government has carefully avoided the issue of how much it will cost to put right these wrongs. The failure to look after returning, often traumatised troops leads to yet further hidden costs to the US economy: the consequences of unemployment, family violence, crime, alcoholism and drug abuse, for example.

The projected $2.5trn price tag also includes the costs of replacing and replenishing military equipment in use. Nearly 40 per cent of the army's equipment, according to the *Washington Post*, is currently deployed in Iraq; as long ago as March 2005, Rumsfeld conceded that tanks, fighting vehicles and helicopters were wearing out at six times the normal rate.

Significant quantities of equipment are being destroyed, too. The *Washington Post* reported last December that the army alone has lost more than 280,000 major pieces of equipment in the combat zones; the *Army Times* reported as long ago as February last year that 20 M1 Abram tanks, 50 Bradley fighting vehicles, 20 Stryker wheeled combat vehicles, 20 M113 armoured personnel carriers, 250 Hum vees, hundreds of mine-clearing vehicles and the like—plus more than a hundred aircraft, most of them helicopters—have been lost. Those figures have increased considerably since then as fighting has intensified. Add something between $125bn and $300bn for *these* unanticipated long-term costs, say Bilmes and Stiglitz.

Yet another gargantuan White House miscalculation was over the price of oil. Before his departure, Larry Lindsey told the *Wall Street Journal* in September 2002 that "the successful prosecution of the war would be good for the economy"; the *WSJ* echoed his thoughts in an editorial the same day, arguing that "the best way to keep oil prices in check is a short, successful war on Iraq". In 2002, the average cost of a barrel of oil was $23.71; today, it is hovering around $50. Dick Cheney's chums in firms such as his own Halliburton—or ExxonMobil, Shell, BP and Chevron—have profited enormously, but Bilmes estimates that even if only $5 of the oil-price increase can be attributed to the Iraq war, that alone adds $150bn to the cost of war.

In the dispassionate way economists assess such things, Bilmes and Stiglitz estimate the additional cost to the economy of the death of a young soldier—typically 25 years old—to be $6.5m.

There are also countless imponderables that add to the bill. The deployment of hundreds of thousands of reservists depletes the economy. At present, 44 per cent of US police forces, for example, have members deployed as reservists in Iraq, and their duties have to be performed by others in America; the same goes for firefighters, medical staff, prison wardens.

Then there are the *future* illnesses that may well unfold. For instance, nobody knew that the notorious Agent Orange defoliant, used by the US in Vietnam from 1961–71, would turn out to have had carcinogenic and other effects on US troops. Today, there is mounting evidence that exposure to depleted uranium—used for firing anti-tank rounds from US

M1 tanks and A-10 attack aircraft—can cause cancer, diabetes and birth defects. Many veterans are returning to the US with their health apparently in ruins from adverse reactions to anti-anthrax injections and/or consumption of experimental pills to counter chemical warfare agents. The long-term costs of looking after the likes of them make the cost of the actual war dead pale by comparison: spouses of deceased soldiers receive a "death gratuity" of $100,000. Troops are also given the opportunity to take out subsidised life insurance policies for up to $500,000 for dependants. In the dispassionate way economists assess such things, Bilmes and Stiglitz estimate the additional cost to the economy of the death of a young soldier—typically 25 years old—to be $6.5m.

Bilmes has become a marked woman to the Bush administration. She was invited to participate in a VA seminar on the cost of war, to be held on the last day of this month—but then was suddenly uninvited. She is no raving lefty, though, and her economic credentials are unimpeachable: she was responsible for an annual budget of $9bn in the Clinton-era commerce department. Like none other than George W Bush, she, too, holds an MBA from Harvard.

It is sobering to think how the money going down the drain in Iraq could otherwise have been spent. "For this amount of money, we could have provided health insurance for the uninsured of this country," Bilmes tells me. "We could have made social security solvent for the next three generations, and implemented all the 9/11 Commission's recommendations [to tighten domestic security]."

That kind of list goes on: the annual cost of treating all heart disease and diabetes in the United States would amount to a quarter of what the Iraq war is costing. Pre-school for every child in America would take just $35bn a year. In their main paper, Bilmes and Stiglitz come up with an even more intriguing possibility: "We could have had a Marshall Plan for the Middle East, or the developing countries, that might have succeeded in winning hearts and minds."

What a historic triumph that would have been for Bush. Instead, his legacy to generations of Americans will be a needless debt of at least $2.5trn, what his own defence secretary describes as a four-way civil war in Iraq, dangerous instability in the Middle East, and increasingly entrenched hatred of the United States throughout the world. Alas, we are likely to hear the daily roar of those C-17s as they approach Andrews Air Force Base for years to come. . . .

12

The Military Is Losing Ground in Its Battle Against Soldier Suicides

Halimah Abdullah

Halimah Abdullah is a political reporter. In addition to the Lexington Herald-Leader, *she has written for the* New York Times, Newsday *and the* Dallas Morning News.

The military's suicide rate, which historically has been lower than that of the general population, has been rising steadily. In 2009 there were 160 active-duty suicides, up from 140 in 2008. Suicide rates among recently-returned veterans are also on the rise. The Department of Defense and the Department of Veterans Affairs have begun to openly address the stigma attached to seeking assistance for mental health problems. They now encourage soldiers and veterans to seek help while dealing with the "invisible wounds" of the wars in Iraq and Afghanistan.

Eight years of war in Afghanistan and Iraq have etched indelible scars on the psyches of many of the nation's servicemen and women, and the U.S. military is losing a battle to stem an epidemic of suicides in its ranks.

Despite calls by top Pentagon officials for a sea change in attitudes about mental health, millions of dollars in new suicide prevention programming and thousands of hours spent helping soldiers suffering from what often are called "invisible wounds," the military is losing ground.

The Department of Defense reported this month [January 2010] there were 160 reported active-duty Army suicides in 2009, up from 140 in 2008.

"There's no question that 2009 was a painful year for the Army when it came to suicides," Col. Christopher Philbrick, deputy director of the Army Suicide Prevention Task Force, said in a statement, despite what he called "wide-ranging measures last year to confront the problem."

While the military's suicide rate is comparable to civilian rates, the increase last year is alarming because the armed services traditionally had lower suicide rates than the general population did.

"I look at the numbers of each service, and that rate has gone up at the same rate across the services," Adm. Mike Mullen, chairman of the Joint Chiefs of Staff, told a recent gathering of military mental health professionals and advocates. "This isn't just a ground force problem."

Some of the suicides are young men, fresh from deployments and haunted by memories, who shoot themselves after they return from their second or third tours in Iraq or Afghanistan, or when romantic relationships turn sour.

Others are career officers who quietly nurse addictions to drugs or alcohol, and decide to silence their ghosts.

The emotional wounds are so deep and the suicide rates are so high that top Pentagon officials ... have started speaking publicly and vehemently about the effects of mental illness.

An increasing number are female troops, who rarely committed suicide before but now are killing themselves at a much higher rate.

"There does not appear to be any scientific correlation between the number of deployments and those that are at risk, but I'm just hard pressed to believe that's not the case," Mullen said.

The emotional wounds are so deep and the suicide rates are so high that top Pentagon officials broke a generations-long code of silence on the topic and have started speaking publicly and vehemently about the effects of mental illness.

The military's shift in attitudes was evident earlier this month during a joint Departments of Defense [DoD] and Veterans Affairs [VA] suicide prevention conference, where uniformed attendees spoke about the stigma of seeking mental health care, the need for policy changes that will make help easier to get and the importance of supporting the families of troops suffering from mental illness.

"It's a joint DoD and VA conference; that alone says an awful lot about where we used to be and where we are now," Mullen said.

Fort Campbell's Fight

With one of the highest suicide rates in the Army, Fort Campbell, a sprawling installation on the Kentucky-Tennessee line that's home to the elite 101st Airborne Division, illustrates the severity of the problem.

In 2007, Fort Campbell created a suicide task force after nine soldiers killed themselves, three during the first few weeks of October.

"As our soldiers fight terrorism, the sacrifices asked of them and their families have increased significantly," the 101st Airborne's commander, Maj. Gen. Jeffrey Schloesser, said in a letter to troops. "Regrettably, under such circumstances, it is natural for our people to feel the stress of these demands and to be overwhelmed at times. Tragically, these pressures too often end in suicide."

The following year, Fort Campbell's suicide rate jumped to 12.

The base hired a suicide prevention program manager and dispatched staffers to study trends, increased awareness training for troops and boosted the number of mental health professionals available to soldiers while in combat and after they return. Army officials say those efforts could prove useful servicewide.

Last year, Fort Campbell held a three-day "suicide standdown," and top officials pleaded with soldiers to get help if they needed it assuring them that seeking help wasn't a sign of weakness and wouldn't affect their careers.

The number of suicides increased to 14 in 2009.

"It's been discouraging to say the least," said Joe Varney, the suicide prevention program manager.

Mixed Messages

Stemming the rise in suicides will take more than conferences, task forces, training and studies, said Col. Elspeth Ritchie, director of behavioral health for the Office of the Army Surgeon General. The military also will have to grapple with the easy availability of handguns, a topic that's sure to be unpopular, she said.

"It's amazing to me when you see Fort Campbell, which is at the top of suicide lists. They have a beautiful gun shop in the middle" of the Post Exchange, Ritchie said. "I'm troubled by what I see as a mixed message."

We cannot change stigma until we change policies that contribute to stigma.

Some soldiers who receive counseling are still committing suicide, and many think—with good reason, given previous military policies and attitudes about mental health—that seeking treatment could ruin careers, she said.

"We cannot change stigma until we change policies that contribute to stigma," Ritchie said. "In many ways we talk out of both sides of our mouths."

The Obama administration, at the behest of a small bipartisan congressional group that includes Rep. Hal Rogers, R-Somerset, is reviewing a longstanding unofficial policy that bars the president from sending condolence letters to families of service members who commit suicide.

Family members of soldiers who've committed suicide said changing the policy would go a long way toward removing the stigma because the military already provides a full military burial for soldiers who commit suicide.

13

The Military Response to Soldiers Experiencing Stress Is Changing

Richard Mauer

Richard Mauer is a reporter for the Anchorage Daily News.

Military leaders have begun to review and change a policy which prevents veterans who have committed suicide from being buried with full military honors. The change is part of a broad-based effort to remove the stigma that many in the military feel is associated with seeking help for mental health problems. These efforts are a response to rapidly increasing rates of suicide among actively deployed troops as well as veterans.

No bugler played Taps for Staff Sgt. Anthony S. Schmachtenberger.

There was no gun salute, no fallen soldier display of boots, rifle and helmet—the traditional Army honors for a lost comrade. When a memorial service was held in the Fort Richardson chapel for Schmachtenberger last August [2009], there was only a photograph of the soldier in uniform, propped on an easel.

Schmachtenberger was a 30-year-old paratrooper from Constantinople, Ohio. He enlisted in 1999 and served three deployments to Afghanistan and Iraq. He went over twice with Fort Bragg's 82nd Airborne after 9/11. He was an artilleryman with Fort Richardson's 4-25th Brigade Combat Team when it went to Iraq in 2006 on its surge-extended 14-month mission.

He was not killed in battle. He died alone July 29 on the garage floor of his East Anchorage duplex apartment. He was found with his head resting on a folded blanket, a half-consumed alcohol bottle nearby and his pickup idling beside him. When the police arrived, the carbon monoxide level was so deadly they feared for the people in the next-door unit until they learned it was rented by another soldier, then in Afghanistan.

Soldier Was One of Three Last Year

Schmachtenberger was one of three Fort Richardson soldiers to kill themselves in 2009, the local manifestation of a growing epidemic of suicides among America's battle-stressed military.

But the failure of the commanders of his own artillery battalion to give him final military honors may have been symptomatic of another aspect of the epidemic: the stigma put on soldiers who show signs of mental stress.

When you do a memorial service in a different way (for a suicide victim), I think that you're adding to the stigmatization of a soldier who has a behavioral health problem.

"It sends the wrong message," Maj. Gen. William Troy, the commander of the Army in Alaska, said in a recent interview.

"When you do a memorial service in a different way (for a suicide victim), I think that you're adding to the stigmatization of a soldier who has a behavioral health problem. You don't mean to, but what you're doing is, you're making it look like it's his fault," Troy said. "We should be memorializing his service to the nation, his service in combat. He's a volunteer, a member of a free nation who came and joined our ranks to defend this country and that's what we should be memorializing, not passing judgment on the manner of his death."

Military Leaders Know That Change Is Needed

Over the past year, the Army's top leaders have been increasingly emphasizing that the stigma must end if soldiers are to believe they can seek mental health therapy without fearing it will ruin their Army careers or bring personal ridicule. Pushing that message down through the ranks to battalion, company, platoon and squad leaders remains one of their big challenges, they say.

Changing that aspect of military culture is especially critical in Alaska now. The 4,500-troop 1-25th Stryker brigade returned late last summer from Iraq to Fort Wainwright in Fairbanks. It has just begun to rebuild for its next assignment.

The 3,500 paratroopers of the 4-25th airborne brigade are on the way home to Fort Richardson this month after a year in a dangerous corner of Afghanistan. Thousands of additional soldiers, reservists and members of the National Guard in Alaska are regularly rotating through the two theaters.

And it's not just a problem facing active-duty personnel. The problems often persist when soldiers return to civilian life. Alaska has the highest percentage of veterans in its population of any state.

The Army once had a lower suicide rate than the civilian population, adjusted for age and gender. But the rate has been climbing steadily since the wars in Afghanistan and Iraq, and is now higher than among civilians. The rates are climbing in the three other military services as well.

Last month, the Army reported that 160 soldiers killed themselves in 2009, up from 140 the previous year.

Fort Rich reported no suicides from 2003 to 2007. There was one reported case in 2008 and three in 2009.

But there might have been more. The body of a soldier just back from Iraq in July 2008 was found on the roof of a Ship Creek warehouse below the A Street-C Street Bridge. With neither witnesses nor note, Anchorage police couldn't determine whether he jumped or fell. He was not listed among the suicides.

Troy assumed his command at Fort Rich on Sept. 11, about a month after Schmachtenberger's memorial. Before his arrival, battalion or brigade commanders in Alaska decided how to conduct a final service.

"It's not up to them anymore," Troy said. The case that changed the rules involved a Stryker brigade soldier in Fort Wainwright who died in his barracks room Sept. 2, four days after returning from Iraq. The soldier's death was still under investigation by the military at the time; suicide was a possibility, though it has since been ruled an accident.

"It was one of the first questions I was asked when I was here—did I want memorials done in a different way for suicides? I said absolutely not," Troy said.

Emotional Distress Should Not Be Stigmatized

Pvt. Tim Gaestel was a new soldier when he arrived at the 82nd Airborne's headquarters at Fort Bragg, N.C., in 2002. Schmachtenberger, then a specialist, a few ranks above private, befriended him.

"He was the ideal person to meet because he didn't mess around—he told you what the Army was going to be like for a private," Gaestel said in a telephone interview last fall from his home in Austin, Texas, where he is now out of the service and attending college.

"He was the biggest class clown, always making jokes, but when it was time to be serious, he was there," Gaestel said.

Gaestel deployed twice with Schmachtenberger in C Battery of the 1st Battalion, 319th Airborne Field Artillery Regiment. During their tour in Iraq, the brother of one of their buddies committed suicide. While their friend was gone for the funeral, he and Schmachtenberger sat out on the dunes, talking about suicide.

"It was never an option for him," Gaestel said. "It was always like, 'Man, I feel bad for Jamie, but still, I would never ever kill myself—I could never do that.'"

Gaestel left the Army after the second deployment, but Schmachtenberger stayed on, following his dream of a career as a soldier, Gaestel said. The two were part of a circle of active duty soldiers and vets who stayed in touch by e-mails and text messages. Schmachtenberger went to Iraq again with his new Fort Rich battalion from October 2006 to December 2007.

Gaestel was surprised to learn Schmachtenberger didn't deploy for a fourth time when his Fort Rich unit, the 2nd Battalion, 377th Parachute Field Artillery Regiment, went to Afghanistan in February 2009. Schmachtenberger stayed behind in the battalion's rear detachment.

"No matter what, Tony would want to go. That's how he was," Gaestel said.

Schmachtenberger's mother, Robin Scalero of Alliance, Ohio, said Schmachtenberger indeed wanted to go, but had broken his pelvis and couldn't function as a paratrooper.

Schmachtenberger attempted suicide in his track several weeks before he succeeded, Scalero said. She wonders why he wasn't hospitalized or put on suicide watch.

Still, Schmachtenberger seemed OK, she said in a telephone interview. When his half-brother—Scalero's youngest son—attempted suicide in January after getting out of the Army, Schmachtenberger's reaction was similar to what Gaestel saw in the dunes.

"Tony jumped all over him, told him how immature it was, and that he can better himself," Scalero said.

"And then Anthony does this in July."

Schmachtenberger attempted suicide in his truck several weeks before he succeeded, Scalero said. She wonders why he wasn't hospitalized or put on suicide watch.

Some of their mutual friends think problems he was having with his second wife had caused him stress, Gaestel said, but that doesn't explain everything.

"He's previously been divorced, and I watched that relationship crumble, and the whole time Tony had his head up," Gaestel said.

Gaestel has been counseling vets at school, and has seen some of this before.

"When you deal with death like a soldier does, then taking your own life, it doesn't feel the same way," Gaestel said. "That's the only thing I can think of, that Tony experienced some really bad stuff and then was thrown some bad stuff."

It will be a mammoth task for the Army to convince career soldiers that it's OK to admit to suffering from stress and accept therapy or counseling, Gaestel said.

"You're supposed to be a man. Yeah, war is hell, but get over it," Gaestel said. "There's no way that you could stay in the military, become a career soldier, and ever go and say, 'I have problems.' As much as they claim you wouldn't, you would be shunned from your unit. Anytime you'd go to a board (for a promotion) there'd be four first sergeants that would all know what happened.

"When I first got to the 82nd Airborne, it was just common knowledge that if somebody went crazy, they go to the sixth floor of the hospital there. For the rest of the time I was in the Army, anybody who was feeling depressed, they were like, 'Watch out, you might end up on the sixth floor.' It was a very negative connotation with seeking any mental health treatment or anything like that."

The New Program at Fort Richardson

Maj. Gen. Troy, the Alaska commander, acknowledges that it's not enough to tell soldiers they should seek counseling when they need it. They need to see that it has no negative impact on their careers, he said.

"We are trying to convince people in the military, in the Army, that it is a sign of strength, not a sign of weakness, when you care enough about yourself, your family and your buddies to see that you got a problem that you need help with, then go seek that help," he said. "There's not a contradiction between being mentally tough on the battlefield and realizing you've been through a tremendously traumatic experience that you may need help with."

Troy cited the example of a four-star general, Carter Ham, who went public in 2009 with the depression and post-traumatic stress he suffered four years earlier from a difficult deployment in Mosul, Iraq. He's now commander of U.S. forces in Europe.

It's not enough to tell soldiers they should seek counseling when they need it. They need to see that it has no negative impact on their careers.

In a visit to Fort Rich in December, Gen. Peter Chiarelli, the Army's vice chief of staff, told Troy and his brigade commanders that they've got to "decrease this stigma," Troy said.

The soldiers returning to Fort Rich this month from Afghanistan will be the first from a brigade-size unit to test a new mental health program designed to do just that. The Virtual Behavioral Health Pilot Program will screen every 4-25th soldier from the commander, Col. Michael Howard, and his sergeant major down to each private. First they'll describe their experiences in a questionnaire, including any traumatic brain injury they might have suffered, then enter a booth for a private video conference with a mental health professional.

The on-line professional can make an immediate referral, including appointment, with a local counselor or therapist, Troy said.

The program showed promise when it was tested on a unit of about 700 soldiers in Hawaii, and Army officials are anxious to try it with a full brigade, Troy said.

Officials believe there are enough mental health professionals in Anchorage to cope with the influx. Health-care companies with military contracts have been building mailing lists from the license files of Alaska therapists, sending out job offers for work with soldiers and their families.

Brenda Moore, chairwoman of the Alaska Suicide Prevention Council, said she's concerned about Alaska's rural areas, where veterans, national guardsmen and reservists live but where there are few mental health providers.

"Our suicide rate, especially among our Native male population, is five times the national rate, which is already a problem. Add to that the kinds of things that some have now experienced on the battlefield, and that adds more to the problem," she said. "We know that this is going to add a whole other level of need out there, and how to meet it is the million dollar question. We know that we have workforce issues, we know we have funding issues."

As a member of the Senate's Armed Services and Veterans Affairs committees, U.S. Sen. Mark Begich said the Army has been making progress, but added: "We've got to do more here."

"The mental stress is enormous now," Begich, D-Alaska, said in a telephone interview. "We're just seeing the beginnings of a prolonged engagement, both in Afghanistan and Iraq, and the results that will be paid for, for many, many, many years."

The connection between traumatic brain injury and suicide became quite personal for Begich as a result of a subcommittee hearing he attended on April 29 on post-traumatic stress disorder. Among the witnesses were retired Army Lt. Col. Raymond Rivas and his wife, Colleen. Rivas suffered multiple concussions in Iraq and was having a serious time coping.

Begich said Rivas looked physically fit but had trouble speaking. His wife explained how she had given up her life to care for him.

We cannot just assume we are doing a good job [of caring for the wounded]—we have to excel in this. . . .

"As I sat there, her testimony was riveting about her struggles supporting her soldier," Begich said.

Two and half months later, Rivas killed himself.

"We cannot just assume we are doing a good job—we have to excel in this," Begich said.

A Tragic Mistake

Spec. Steven Griffis sought help at Fort Richardson after he and his wife Lacy, also a soldier, returned from a 10-month deployment to Iraq July 4, 2007. They were in C Company of the 864th Engineer Combat Battalion (Heavy).

Steven Griffis, then 21, from West Palm Beach, Fla., operated a HEMTT—a huge armored tow truck used to recover American Humvees and other vehicles wrecked in roadside bombs to keep them out of the hands of insurgents. Lacy Griffis, then 22, was the quartermaster who supplied the motor pools.

Lacy Griffis said her husband's job required him to go on convoys about every other day they were in Iraq. He was shot at and he shot back. Though he wasn't injured, he would have to clean up the bloody aftermath of a bomb attack on an American vehicle, she said.

"It affects you," said his father, Steven Griffis Sr., a carpenter from Florida. "When he got back to Alaska, he was asking for some help, and the command was just kind of pacifying him."

Lacy Griffis said she thinks the Army medical personnel mistook a bipolar condition for attention deficit disorder and prescribed medication that made him worse. Her husband's mother died from complications associated with a bipolar disorder, she said.

Her company, with about 145 soldiers, seven of them female, had its share of woes, she said. There was Pvt. 1st Class Edward Byrnes, 36, from Limerick, Ireland, the soldier who jumped or fell from a bridge on First Avenue July 11, 2008. Spec. Blake Bronaugh, 22, from Wichita Falls, Tex., died in his barracks room that Thanksgiving Day. Several other soldiers attempted suicide but were rescued, Lacy Griffis said.

Around January 2009, the Griffis were living off-base in an apartment in Eagle River. He began talking about suicide. They would argue. She spoke to some sergeants and they agreed to take her husband's personal weapons: a .44-magnum revolver and shotgun.

Army medical personnel mistook a bipolar condition for attention deficit disorder and prescribed medication that made him worse.

Stress Can Have Many Sources

On March 18, the couple was attending a marriage counseling session on Fort Rich. Lacy Griffis said hurtful words were spoken, then her husband told her she had messed up and ran from the room. She immediately called her squad leader, who asked if her husband had his weapons.

"As far as I know, no," she replied. The squad leader called Steven Griffis' sergeant. He found out the weapons had been returned because Griffis had been acting more stable. The squad leader called Lacy Griffis back with the bad news. She wanted to race home but was told to stay on base.

"They were afraid he was going to kill me instead of himself," she said. She called the MPs [military police] at the entrance to the base, but Griffis had just left and they had no jurisdiction in Eagle River. She called Anchorage Police.

"I was hysterical. I was like, 'I want someone there right now, right now, right now.'" The dispatcher tried to calm her. "I was like, 'I'm not calming down until there's someone there breaking down my damn door.'"

A good friend of Griffis raced toward Eagle River, too. As he drove, he was texting Griffis.

"You aren't going to hurt ur self r u?" the friend wrote, according to an Anchorage police report.

"Sorry," was Griffis' reply.

When Anchorage police arrived, Griffis was inside and the friend outside. Anchorage Police Officer Justin Voss tried to call Griffis, but he didn't answer.

The cops got the key to the apartment and crawled in. Voss reported seeing the boots of a soldier at the top of a flight of stairs. The soldier's right forearm was pointing in the direction of his own head.

Griffis' home phone was ringing. No one answered. When the answering machine came on, Voss heard a female voice urging Griffis to open the door for police.

Voss called to Griffis, then heard a gunshot. Griffis tumbled down the stairs, still alive but shot through the head. He died on the way to the hospital.

Over the summer, Lacy Griffis got a reassignment to a base in the South.

"Both of us were incredibly stressed out, pretty much all the time," she said. Some of it was their relationship, but their deployment and their jobs also played a big part, she said.

"There was just so much going on and there was just one thing right after the other."

14

Condolences Should Go to Families of Soldiers Who Commit Suicide

Michael Blumenfield

Michael Blumenfield, MD, is The Sidney E. Frank Distinguished Professor Emeritus of Psychiatry and Behavioral Sciences at New York Medical College.

The President of the United States writes letters of condolence to the families of soldiers who are killed during their military service. However, it is an unwritten policy that families of soldiers who commit suicide do not receive letters from the president. This policy demeans the service and sacrifice of those who have died, and it causes pain to families who have suffered a great loss. Every soldier should be honored for his or her service. Families of soldiers who kill themselves should receive a letter from the president, stating that the service of their loved one was valued.

When a soldier is killed while in the military service the President writes a condolence letter to the family. However, if a soldier is psychologically injured and then commits suicide, there is no Presidential letter of condolence. There is apparently an unwritten policy that this does not include families of soldiers who have committed suicide.

It is easy to imagine how hurtful that must be for families who are burying a loved one who came back from war with psychological problems and then committed suicide or perhaps did it overseas.

One Family's Story

After my blog on this subject appeared in PsychiatryTalk.com I received a comment from Gregg Keesling the father of one such soldier and then had a correspondence with him. His story was also written up in the *NY Times*. His 25-year-old son Chancellor served two deployments. He committed suicide in Iraq after sending his parents an email telling them of his decision. He said that "military investigations demonstrated, our son Chancellor was a good soldier. He succumbed to an illness as much as someone who dies in the war theater from food poisoning or infection, and we believe that the President should send condolences and express the country's appreciation of our family's sacrifice." A spokesperson for President Obama said that the policy in regard to who should receive a letter of condolence is currently undergoing a review.

Why Would the President Not Send Condolences?

I have tried to understand why anyone would advocate that the President should not express condolence to families such as the Keeslings. I heard one view that many soldiers would feel that their comrade's combat death would be demeaned if the families of soldiers who suicided were given an equal letter of condolence. Another view is that treating suicide the same as other war deaths might encourage mentally frail soldiers to take their lives by making the act seem honorable. I believe these ideas are misguided and resurrect the stigmatization of mental illness. Soldiers cannot will themselves to avoid these emotional states anymore than a soldier can avoid a bullet or an explosive device. Once you are in a combat zone, you are vulnerable to injury. I know of no evidence that people on the verge of suicide would be driven to it because their family would get a letter of condolence.

They Are All Heroes

If a soldier in Iraq were accidentally killed in a car accident, would his death be any less deserving a letter of condolence than a soldier who was killed in an enemy ambush? Would the family be any less deserving of the letter if the soldier made a tactical error leading to his death as compared to someone who bravely fell on a grenade to save others lives? Similarly, would you compare a soldier who faced many horrific combat situations and developed PTSD [Post Traumatic Stress Disorder] with another soldier who became severely depressed shortly after arrival in the combat zone if both ended up having intolerable suicidal feelings, which led to their death? I don't believe that we judge some soldiers' deaths as being more worthy than others. Yes, we do give out medals for unusual acts of bravery but this in no way diminishes the sacrifices that others have made. Every soldier has volunteered and knows that he or she could be exposed to combat. For this they deserve our thanks and when they make the supreme sacrifice, their families deserve a letter of condolence.

I don't believe that we judge some soldiers' death as being more worthy than others.

Recent Actions to Attempt to Influence the President

On December 23rd [2009] a bipartisan coalition of 44 House members initiated by Reps Patrick Kennedy and Dan Burton sent a letter to President Obama. They wrote "By overturning this policy on letters of condolence to the families of suicide victims you can send a strong signal that you will not tolerate a culture in our Armed Forces that discriminates against those with a mental illness." The American Foundation for Suicide Prevention in a letter to the President on January 5th wrote "We agree with members of Congress that you can send a strong signal that you will not tolerate a culture in our military services that discriminates against those with mental illness. Please Mr. President, overturn this policy as soon as possible." On January 7th Mental Health American announced the adoption of a position requesting the President revoke the policy of not writing condolence letters to families of soldiers who have committed suicide They also started an online petition on Facebook.

I continue to urge anyone concerned about this issue to write to the President. Those who are mental health professionals should state this and explain your views based on your understanding of mental illness.

15

Condolences Should Not Go to Families of Soldiers Who Commit Suicide

Paul Steinberg

Paul Steinberg is a psychiatrist and a former director of the counseling and psychiatric service at Georgetown University.

The question of whether the President of the United States should send letters of condolence to the families of soldiers who commit suicide is complex. Suicide has historically been considered a sin and a crime, and copycat suicides demonstrate that a single act of suicide that is publicized can lead others to commit similar acts. Thus, in deciding whether he should write letters of condolence to the families of suicides, the president must balance the needs of the family against issues of public health.

The recent revelation that the families of service members who are suicides do not receive presidential condolence letters created a stir, evoking questions of fairness and raising concerns about a lack of compassion from our leaders.

Yet the issue is far more complicated than that. Indeed, there is nothing wrong with stigmatizing suicide while doing everything possible to de-stigmatize the help soldiers need in dealing with post-traumatic stress and suicidal thoughts.

The key question is to what extent any action we take after a suicide inadvertently glorifies it. Early Christians realized that they were losing too many believers to the attractions of

Paul Steinberg, "Obama's Condolence Problem," *New York Times*, December 12, 2009. Copyright © 2008 Paul Steinberg MD. Reprinted with permission.

martyrdom. A halt to this epidemic of provoking martyrdom by suicide was brought about in the fourth century when St. Augustine codified the church's disapproval of suicide and condemned the taking of one's own life as a grievous sin.

Canonical law ultimately pushed civil law in too harsh a direction. Only in 1961 did England repeal its law making suicide a crime. As late as 1974 in the United States, suicide was still considered a crime in eight states.

The key question is to what extent any action we take after a suicide inadvertently glorifies it.

Has the pendulum swung too far in the other direction? Now that first-rate treatments for depression and post-traumatic stress have evolved and are readily available, and people with emotional problems do not have to suffer quietly, are we taking away the shame of suicide?

Copycat Suicides Are a Danger

For more than 30 years, we in the mental-health field have been aware of the prevalence of copycat suicides. Whenever the news of a well-known figure killing himself hits the front pages, a significant bump in suicides, reflecting copycat deaths, invariably follows in the next few days. Strikingly, there is no corresponding decline in suicides in the weeks after this bump—forcing us to conclude that the victims are people who would not have otherwise killed themselves.

The hard truth is that any possible glorification of suicide—even reports of suicide—make the taking of one's life a more viable option. If suicide appears to be a more reasonable way of handling life's stresses than seeking help, then suicide rates increase.

Certainly, a presidential condolence letter after one's death is not exactly the same encouragement for suicide as the purported Muslim promise of a gift of 72 virgins after death. But the increasing number of suicides in the military suggests that we need to find the right balance between concern for the spouses, children and parents left behind, and any efforts to prevent subsequent suicides in the military.

If suicide appears to be a more reasonable way of handling life's stresses than seeking help, then suicide rates increase.

As a psychiatrist formerly working on college campuses, I, along with my colleagues, was concerned with how we handled the funerals and aftermaths of even accidental deaths of students. Compassion for those left behind arose naturally; at the same time, we did not want to glorify the death to a point that lonely, distressed students might consider death better than life.

A difficult balancing act, to be sure. For people under 30, suicide is highly correlated with impulsivity and suggestibility. Thus college campuses and military installations, with their young populations, must be particularly aware of the possibility of copycat suicides and the dangers of a veneration of death.

President Obama, as commander in chief, has to balance the wishes of families with the demands of public health. In light of the condolence-letter controversy, the administration is appropriately reviewing the policy that has been in place for at least 17 years—and may indeed want to consider leaving it as it is. But as a country, let's focus our energies on doing everything we can to diminish inadvertent incentives that might increase self-inflicted deaths.

16

Casualties of the War on Terror Have Made a Military Welfare State

Gordon Duff

Gordon Duff is a Marine Vietnam veteran, grunt and 100% disabled vet. He has been a United Nations diplomat and a defense contractor and is a widely published expert on military and defense issues.

The costs of war are enormous, and will bankrupt the U.S. Large numbers of disabled veterans from the "War on Terror" will be claiming disability checks for their entire lives. Additionally, health care for their families and tuition for their children all add up enormously, over $300,000 for a typical family. However, the will to keep promises to veterans, and the funds to pay for them, do not exist. Historically, the government has found ways to avoid paying for the real costs of war, and it will do the same this time.

Vietnam should have been a lesson but we don't learn, not when money is involved. In a war with no civilian contractors and a much lower combat/support ratio in theatre, casualty levels were more than ten times higher than during the "War on Terror." The lessons were there, tens of thousands of suicides and less than half of Vietnam veterans lived to 60 years old. Percentage figures, combat or support, dead, disabled, homeless, prison, divorce, illness and death, always a figure everyone can understand, all avoided like the plague. Ask no questions, suffer no knowledge.

We did it again. We are blaming the Department of Veterans Affairs for our failures. Who do you think tells them to shred millions of documents or deny disability claims until veterans are dead? As with Social Security, disability pensions for disabled vets from Vietnam started kicking in after decades of ignoring illnesses, misdiagnosing problems, destroying paperwork and watching veterans die in poverty, with the children of most Vietnam veterans suffering the most.

Why continually send us to war if we aren't willing to pay the bills?

500,000 "War on Terror" Veterans

While Vietnam veterans began receiving disability in their 50's, younger veterans apply for disability immediately. Instead of a year or two of disability, they will live their entire lives as "disabled veterans." The numbers are the telling part. It is estimated we are going to have 500,000 "War on Terror" veterans receiving disability for decades, with full health insurance for their families, tuition for their children and more. A typical family with 2 kids in college will cost well over $100,000 between disability, medical care, tuition, dependents allowances and fees with that figure going to over $300,000 when VA [Veterans Administration] processing and management costs are taken into account.

This is why the GOP [Grand Old Party/Republican Party] has typically voted against veteran issues. They are going to bankrupt the country. My question is, why continually send us to war if we aren't willing to pay the bills?

When considering what has been done to our military, not only those serving but veterans and the general awareness that the promise of training, a steady job and a "fair deal" is untrue, our current wars have done more to damage our overall national security than we will ever be able to gauge. . . .

The Lives of a Generation Have Been Destroyed

With 500,000 "breadwinners" as disabled veterans, essentially half a million young families, ripped out of our economy, eating more money than national health care, Federal aid to education, food stamps and all American foreign aid combined, we are building a "military welfare state" inside the United States that will go on forever. Service in our current military, with constant deployments and lives interrupted for a decade has left the majority of those who served as ineffective soldiers, unemployable private citizens and, in many cases, permanent patients requiring a lifetime of physical or psychological treatment at a staggering cost.

Attempts to curtail this problem, attempts that have cost hundreds of millions of dollars, have been totally ineffective; in fact, our military is "melting down" at an increasingly rapid rate.

Our Government's "Back Stabbing" Solutions

Cutting back on the costs of our wars and our foreign policy meant more to serve others than ourselves has required some creativity on the part of our military and government. One of the favored ploys of the military is to hand out bad discharges whenever possible, especially to troops who are suffering from severe PTSD [Post Traumatic Stress Disorder] and too disabled to function in combat. Some day a dishonorable discharge may be the equivalent of a Medal of Honor, proof someone has sacrificed him or herself for their country "above and beyond the call of duty." If only this were a joke. How many heroes are out there with "bad paper?"

At the civilian level, dealing with "veterans," there are a variety of games from considering any psychological or physical disorder as "pre-existing" to losing paperwork over and over to systematic psychological abuse. This system was proven to work on Vietnam veterans and is deeply engrained into Veterans Affairs.

Destabilization of America: Who Does It Serve?

We have seen economic collapse under massive debt, war, corruption and tax cuts moving us into 3rd world status. We have seen our military exhausted, our manpower base destroyed and disillusioned.

> *We have no intention to care for our veterans, we have no intention to support our troops.*

If the US exhausts itself in decades of war in oil and gas rich Asia and ends up only beset with debt, terrorism and half a dozen new nuclear powers, does this make America the loser? If India and Israel control central Asia, and Russia and China control the world's money supply, what is left for the United States other than to act as a mercenary or dupe? Was there a grand plan at all, aimed at anything other than the destruction of the United States, seemingly at her own hands?

Are we this stupid or is something else at work here?

What is certain is that the will to keep promises and the funds necessary to finance that will, does not exist. We have no intention to care for our veterans, we have no intention to support our troops. The first group to be tossed on the scrap pile has always been and will always be our veterans and soldiers. And so it goes. . . .

17

Casualties from Terrorism Are Minor Compared to Other Threats

Tom Englehardt

Tom Engelhardt is a Fellow of The Nation Institute, and also of the Graduate School of Journalism at the University of California, Berkeley.

The press over-reacted to the attempted bombing of Northwest Airlines Flight 253 on Christmas day 2009, just as it has over-reacted to other purported terrorist events in the past nine years. Since September 11, 2001, fear of terrorism, and of casualties that might be caused by terrorism, have been nurtured and even institutionalized in our society. In reality, the poor economy, job losses and home foreclosures are far greater threats to the lives of Americans.

L et me put American life in the Age of Terror into some kind of context, and then tell me you're not ready to get on the nearest plane heading anywhere, even toward Yemen.

In 2008, 14,180 Americans were murdered, according to the FBI [Federal Bureau of Invesigations]. In that year, there were 34,017 fatal vehicle crashes in the U.S. and, so the U.S. Fire Administration tells us, 3,320 deaths by tire. More than 11,000 Americans died of the swine flu between April and mid-December 2009, according to the Centers for Disease

Control and Prevention; on average, a staggering 443,600 Americans die yearly of illnesses related to tobacco use, reports the American Cancer Society; 5,000 Americans die annually from food-borne diseases; an estimated 1,760 children died from abuse or neglect in 2007; and the next year, 560 Americans died of weather-related conditions, according to the National Weather Service, including 126 from tornadoes, 67 from rip tides, 58 from flash floods, 27 from lightning, 27 from avalanches, and 1 from a dust devil.

As for airplane fatalities, no American died in a crash of a U.S. carrier in either 2007 or 2008, despite 1.5 billion passengers transported. In 2009, planes certainly went down and people died. In June, for instance, a French flight on its way from Rio de Janeiro to Paris disappeared in bad weather over the Atlantic, killing 226. Continental Connection Flight 3407, a regional commuter flight, crashed into a house near Buffalo, New York, that February killing 50, the first fatal crash of a U.S. commercial flight since August 2006. And in January 2009, US Airways Flight 1549, assaulted by a flock of birds, managed a brilliant landing in New York's Hudson River when disaster might have ensued. In none of these years did an airplane go down anywhere due to terrorism, though in 2007 two terrorists smashed a Jeep Cherokee loaded with propane tanks into the terminal of Glasgow International Airport. (No one was killed.)

The now-infamous Northwest Airlines Flight 253 ... had 290 passengers and crew, all of whom survived.

A Story That Was Blown out of Proportion

The now-infamous Northwest Airlines Flight 253, carrying Umar Farouk Abdulmutallab and his bomb-laden underwear toward Detroit on Christmas Day 2009, had 290 passengers and crew, all of whom survived. Had the inept Abdulmutallab actually succeeded, the death toll would not have equaled the 324 traffic fatalities in Nevada in 2008; while the destruction of four Flight 253s from terrorism would not have equaled New York State's 2008 traffic death toll of 1,231, 341 of whom, or 51 more than those on Flight 253, were classified as "alcohol-impaired fatalities."

Had the 23-year-old Nigerian set off his bomb, it would have been a nightmare for the people on board, and a tragedy for those who knew them. It would certainly have represented a safety and security issue that needed to be dealt with. But it would *not* have been a national emergency, nor a national-security crisis. It would have been nothing more than a single plane knocked out of the sky, something that happens from time to time without the intervention of terrorists.

The Media Went Mad

And yet here's the strange thing: thanks to what didn't happen on Flight 253, the media essentially went mad, 24/7. Newspaper coverage of the failed plot and its ramifications actually grew for two full weeks after the incident until it had achieved something like full-spectrum dominance, according to the Pew Research Center's Project for Excellence in Journalism. In the days after Christmas, more than half the news links in blogs related to Flight 253. At the same time, the Republican criticism machine (and the media universe that goes with it) ramped up on the subject of the Obama administration's terror wimpiness; the global air transport system plunked down millions of dollars on new technology which will *not* find underwear bombs; the homeland security-industrial-complex had a field day; and fear, that adrenaline rush from hell, was further embedded in the American way of life.

Under the circumstances, you would never know that Americans living in the United States were in vanishingly little danger from terrorism, but in significant danger driving to the mall; or that alcohol, tobacco, *E. coli bacteria*, fire, domestic abuse, murder, and the weather present the sort of potentially fatal problems that might be worth worrying about, or even changing your behavior over, or perhaps investing some money in. Terrorism, not so much.

The few Americans who, since 2001, have died from anything that could be called a terror attack in the U.S.—whether the 13 killed at Fort Hood or the soldier murdered outside an army recruiting office in Little Rock, Arkansas—were far outnumbered by the 32 dead in a 2007 mass killing at Virginia Tech University, not to speak of the relatively regular moments when workers or former workers "go postal." Since September 11th, terror in the U.S. has rated above fatalities from shark attacks and not much else. Since the economic meltdown of 2008, it has, in fact, been left in the shade by violent deaths that stem from reactions to job loss, foreclosure, inability to pay the rent, and so on.

This is seldom highlighted in a country perversely convulsed by, and that can't seem to get enough of, fantasies about being besieged by terrorists.

The few Americans who, since 2001, have died from anything that could be called a terror attack in the U.S. . . . were far outnumbered by the 32 dead in a 2007 mass killing at Virginia Tech.

Institutionalizing Fear Inc.

The attacks of September 11, 2001, which had the look of the apocalyptic, brought the fear of terrorism into the American bedroom via the TV screen. That fear was used with remarkable effectiveness by the Bush administration, which color-coded terror for its own ends. A domestic version of shock-and-awe—Americans were indeed shocked and awed by 9/11—helped drive the country into two disastrous wars and occupations, each still ongoing, and into George W. Bush's

Global War on Terror, a term now *persona non grata* in Washington, even if the "war" itself goes on and on.

Today, any possible or actual terror attack, any threat no matter how far-fetched, amateurish, poorly executed, or ineffective, raises a national alarm, always seeming to add to the power of the imperial presidency and threatening to open new "fronts" in the now-unnamed global war. The latest is, of course, in Yemen, thanks in part to that young Nigerian who was evidently armed with explosives by a home-grown organization of a few hundred men that goes by the name al-Qaeda in the Arabian Peninsula.

The fear of terrorism has, by now, been institutionalized in our society—quite literally so—even if the thing we're afraid of has, on the scale of human problems, something of the will o' the wisp about it. For those who remember their Cold War fiction, it's more specter than SPECTRE.

Since September 11th, terror in the U.S. has rated above fatalities from shark attacks and not much else.

That fear has been embedded in what once was an un-American word, more easily associated with Soviet Russia or Nazi Germany: "homeland." It has replaced "country," "land," and "nation" in the language of the terror-mongers. "The homeland" is the place which terrorism, and nothing but terrorism, can violate. In 2002, that terror-embedded word got its own official government agency: the Department of Homeland Security, our second "defense" department, which has a 2010 budget of $39.4 billion (while overall "homeland security" spending in the 2010 budget reached $70.2 billion). Around it has grown up a little-attended-to homeland-security complex with its own interests, businesses, associations, and lobbyists (including jostling crowds of ex-politicians and ex-government bureaucrats).

As a result, more than eight years after 9/11, an amorphous state of mind has manifested itself in the actual state as a kind of Fear Inc. A number of factors have clearly gone into the creation of Fear Inc. and now insure that fear is the drug constantly shot into the American body politic. These would include:

The imperial presidency: The Bush administration used fear not only to promote its wars and its Global War on Terror, but also to unchain the commander-in-chief of an already imperial presidency from a host of restraints. The dangers of terror and of al-Qaeda, which became the global bogeyman, and the various proposed responses to it, including kidnapping ("extraordinary rendition"), secret imprisonment, and torture, turned out to be the royal road to the American unconscious and so to a presidency determined, as Secretary of Defense Donald Rumsfeld and others liked to say, to take the gloves off. It remains so and, as a result, under Barack Obama, the imperial presidency only seems to gain ground. Recently, for instance, we learned that, under the pressure of the Flight 253 incident, the Obama administration has adopted the Bush administration position that a president, under certain circumstances, has the authority to order the assassination of an American citizen abroad. (In this case, New Mexico-born Islamic cleric Anwar Aulaqi, who has been linked to the 9/11 plotters, the Fort Hood killer, and Abdulmutallab.) The Bush administration opened the door to this possibility and now, it seems, a Democratic president may be stepping through.

The 24/7 media moment: 24/7 blitz coverage was once reserved for the deaths of presidents (as in the assassination of John F. Kennedy) and public events of agreed-upon import. In 1994, however, it became the coin of the media realm for any event bizarre enough, sensational enough, celebrity-based enough to glue eyeballs. That June, O.J. Simpson engaged in his infamous low-speed car "chase" through Orange County followed by more than 20 news helicopters while 95 million viewers tuned in and thousands more gathered at highway overpasses to watch. No one's ever looked back. Of course, in a traditional media world that's shedding foreign and domestic bureaus and axing hordes of reporters, radically downsizing news rooms and shrinking papers to next to nothing, the advantages of focusing reportorial energies on just one thing at a time are obvious. Those 24/7 energies are now regularly focused on the fear of terrorism and events which contribute to it, like the plot to down Flight 253.

The Republican criticism machine and the media that go with it: Once upon a time, even successful Republican administrations didn't have their own megaphone. That's why, in the Vietnam era, the Nixon administration battled the *New York Times* so fiercely (and—my own guess—that played a part in forcing the creation of the first "op-ed" page in 1970, which allowed administration figures like Vice President Spiro Agnew and ex-Nixon speechwriter William Safire to gain a voice at the paper). By the George W. Bush era, the struggle had abated. The *Times* and papers like it only had to be pacified or cut out of the loop, since from TV to talk radio, publishing to publicity, the Republicans had their own megaphone ready at hand. This is, by now, a machine chock-a-block full of politicians and ex-politicians, publishers, pundits, military "experts," journalists, shock-jocks, and the like (categories that have a tendency to blend into each other). It adds up to a seamless web of promotion, publicity, and din. It's capable of gearing up on no notice and going on until a subject—none more popular than terrorism and Democratic spinelessness in the face of it—is temporarily flogged to death. It ensures that any failed terror attack, no matter how hopeless or pathetic, will be in the headlines and in public consciousness. It circulates constant fantasies about possible future apocalyptic terror attacks with atomic weaponry or other weapons of mass destruction. (And in all of the above, of course, it is helped by a host of tagalong pundits and experts, news shows and news reports from the more liberal side of the aisle.)

The Democrats who don't dare: It's remarkable that the sharpest president we've had in a while didn't dare get up in front of the American people after Flight 253 landed and tell everyone to calm down. He didn't, in fact, have a single intelligent thing to say about the event. He certainly didn't remind Americans that, whatever happened to Flight 253, they stood in far more danger heading out of their driveways behind the wheel or pulling into a bar on the way home for a beer or two. Instead, the Obama administration essentially abjectly apologized, insisted it would focus yet more effort and money on making America safe from air terrorism, widened a new front in the Global War on Terror in Yemen (speeding extra money and U.S. advisors that way), and when the din from its critics didn't end, "pushed back," as Peter Baker of the *New York Times* wrote, by claiming "that they were handling terror suspects much as the previous administration did." It's striking when a Democratic administration finds safety in the claim that it's acting like a Republican one, that it's following the path to the imperial presidency already cleared by George W. Bush. Fear does that to you, and the fear of terror has been institutionalized at the top as well as the bottom of society.

Only a relatively small number of determined fanatics with extraordinarily limited access to American soil keep Fear Inc. afloat.

9/11 Never Ends

Fear has a way of re-ordering human worlds. That only a relatively small number of determined fanatics with extraordinarily limited access to American soil keep Fear Inc. afloat should, by now, be obvious. What the fear machine produces is the dark underside of the charming Saul Steinberg New Yorker cover, "A View of the World from 9th Avenue," in which Manhattan looms vast as the rest of the planet fades into near nothingness.

When you see the world "from 9th Avenue," or from an all-al-Qaeda-all-the-time "news" channel, you see it phantasmagorically. It's out of all realistic shape and proportion, which means you naturally make stupid decisions. You become incapable of sorting out what matters and what doesn't, what's primary and what's secondary. You become, in short, manipulable.

The pin-prick terror events blown up to apocalyptic proportions add up to a second, third, fourth, fifth 9/11 when it comes to American consciousness.

This is our situation today.

People always wonder: What would the impact of a second 9/11-style attack be on this country? Seldom noticed, however, is that all the pin-prick terror events blown up to apocalyptic proportions add up to a second, third, fourth, fifth 9/11 when it comes to American consciousness.

So the next time a Flight 253 occurs and the Republicans go postal, the media morphs into its 24/7 national-security-disaster mode, the pundits register red on the terror-news scale, the president defends himself by reaffirming that he is doing just what the Bush administration would have done, the homeland security lobbyists begin calling for yet more funds for yet more machinery, and nothing much happens, remember those drunken drivers, arsonists, and tobacco merchants, even that single dust devil and say:

Hold onto your underpants, this is *not* a national emergency.

Organizations to Contact

The editors have compiled the following list of organizations concerned with the issues debated in this book. The descriptions are derived from materials provided by the organizations. All have publications or information available for interested readers. The list was compiled on the date of publication of the present volume; the information provided here may change. Be aware that many organizations take several weeks or longer to respond to inquiries, so allow as much time as possible.

American Civil Liberties Union

125 Broad Street, 18⁰ Floor, New York, NY   10004
(212) 549-2666
Email: media@aclu.org
Web site: http://www.aclu.org/

The ACLU is committed to the defense and preservation of individual rights and liberties that are guaranteed by the constitution of the United States of America. The ACLU Web site includes a page of resources about the human costs of war in Iraq and Afghanistan.

The American Legion

700 N. Pennsylvania St., Indianapolis, IN   46206
(317) 630-1200 • FAX: (317) 630-1223
Web site: http://www.legion.org/

The American Legion was chartered and incorporated by Congress in 1919 as a patriotic veterans organization. As the nation's largest veteran-service organization, it mentors and sponsors youth programs, promotes the values of patriotism and honor, advocates for strong national security, and supports programs for veterans and their families.

CIVIC (Campaign for Innocent Victims in Conflict)

1700 Connecticut Ave NW, Washington, DC   20009
(202) 558-6958

Email: info@civicworldwide.org
Web site: http://www.civicworldwide.org/index.php

CIVIC works on behalf of war victims, conducting public advocacy campaigns to persuade parties to conflict to recognize and make amends to civilian casualties of war. It designed a training program for U.S. officers and enlisted forces to reduce civilian casualties in Iraq and Afghanistan. The Making Amends Campaign launched by CIVIC is based on three principles: 1) Civilian suffering in war is a global problem; 2) No survivor of war should be left without recognition and help; and 3) No warring party should be able to simply walk away from the harm it has caused. The CIVIC Web site includes an extensive list of resources on civilian casualties of war.

Defense and Veterans Brain Injury Center

PO Box 59181, Washington, DC   20012
Phone: 202-782-6345
Web site: www.dvbic.org

The mission of the Defense and Veterans Brain Injury Center (DVBIC) is to serve active duty military and veterans with traumatic brain injuries (TBIs) through state-of-the-art clinical care, innovative clinical research initiatives and educational programs. DVBIC fulfills this mission through ongoing collaboration with military, Veterans Administration (VA) and civilian health partners, local communities, families and individuals with TBI. DVBIC has locations at Camp Lejeune, NC, Camp Pendleton, CA, Fort Bragg, NC, Fort Carson, CO, Fort Hood, TX, San Diego, CA, and San Antonio, TX.

Disabled American Veterans

3725 Alexandria Pike, Cold Spring, KY   41076
(877) 426-2838
Web site: https://www.dav.org/Default.aspx

Disabled American Veterans is a non-profit charity dedicated to improving the lives of disabled veterans of the US armed services. It assists veterans in obtaining benefits and services provided by the Department of Veterans Affairs and other government agencies; represents disabled veterans, their spouses and families before Congress, the White House and the Judicial Branch, as well as state and local governments; and provides a structure through which disabled veterans can provide assistance and support to one another.

House Committee on Veterans' Affairs

335 Cannon House Office Building, Washington, DC   20515
(202) 225-9756 • Fax: (202) 225-2034
Web site: http://veterans.house.gov/

The House Committee on Veterans' Affairs is dedicated to improving health care and benefits for veterans of the armed forces of the United States. Subcommittees carry out work on disability assistance and memorial affairs, economic opportunity for veterans, veterans' health care, oversight and investigations.

Human Rights Watch

350 Fifth Avenue, 34⁰ Floor, New York, NY   10118-3299
(212) 290-4700
http://www.hrw.org/

Human Rights Watch (HRW) is an independent organization dedicated to defending and protecting human rights in the international community. It conducts investigations, focuses attention on situations where human rights are being violated, and calls for accountability and justice. The HRW Web site features a News page that often features stories on civilian casualties of war.

The Heritage Foundation

214 Massachusetts Ave NE, Washington, DC   20002-4999
(202) 546-4400
Web site: http://www.heritage.org/

The Heritage Foundation is a conservative think tank whose mission is to promote public policies based on the principles of free enterprise, limited government, individual freedom, traditional American values, and a strong defense. To protect America, the Heritage Foundation believes that the armed forces must have the means to conduct current operations, maintain trained and ready troops, and prepare for the national security challenges of the present and the future.

Institute of Medicine of the National Academies

500 Fifth Street, NW, Washington, DC   20001
(202) 334-2352
Email: iomwww@nas.edu
Web site: http://www.iom.edu/Global/Topics/Veterans-Health.aspx

The Institute of Medicine conducts research to address the health concerns of military personnel and their families both during terms of active duty and after service is completed. Areas of interest include the health effects of military service, readjustment needs of veterans, exposure to uncommon agents and diseases, as well as the transition from health services provided by the Department of Defense to those provided by the Department of Veterans Affairs.

Senate Committee on Veterans Affairs

412 Russell Senate Bldg, Washington, DC   20510
(202) 224-9126
Web site: http://veterans.senate.gov/index.cfm

The Senate Committee on Veterans Affairs has jurisdiction over legislative matters pertaining to the compensation of veterans, life insurance issued by the government for veterans, national cemeteries, pensions, readjustment of servicemen and women to civilian life, veterans' hospitals, medical care of veterans, vocational rehabilitation and education.

The United Nations-UN Headquarters

First Avenue at 46th Street, New York, NY   10017
Web site: http://www.un.org/en/index.shtml

The United Nations is an international organization committed to maintaining international peace and security, developing friendly relations among nations and promoting social progress, better living standards and human rights. The UN engages in peacekeeping, peace-building, conflict prevention and humanitarian assistance. The UN High Commissioner for Human Rights monitors the plight of civilians in war-torn countries. The UN News Service is an additional source of information on the costs of war to civilian populations.

United States Department of Veterans Affairs

810 Vermont Avenue NW, Washington, DC   20420
Web site: http://www.va.gov/

The Department of Veterans Affairs provides a wide range of benefits to veterans of military service including, disability benefits, education and training, vocational rehabilitation and employment, home loan guaranty, dependant and survivor benefits, medical treatment, life insurance and burial benefits. The Department of Veterans Affairs Web site provides comprehensive information on services that are available through the Department of Veterans Affairs.

United States Institute of Peace (USIP)

1200 17th Street NW, Washington, DC   20036
(202) 457-1700 • Fax (202) 429-6063

The United States Institute of Peace is an independent, nonpartisan institution established and funded by Congress. Through research and education it works to help prevent and resolve violent international conflicts, promote post-conflict stability and development and increase conflict management capacity.

Veterans History Project-Library of Congress

101 Independence Ave., SE, Washington, DC   20540
(202) 707-4916 • Fax: (202) 252-2046
Web site: http://www.loc.gov/vets/

The Veterans History Project is part of the American Folklife Center of the Library of Congress. It collects, preserves, and makes accessible the personal accounts of American war veterans so that future generations may hear directly from veterans and better understand the realities of war.

War Resisters League
339 Lafayette Street, New York, NY   10012
(212) 228-0450 • Fax: (2121) 228-6193
Email: wrl@warresisters.org
http://www.warresisters.org/index.php

The War Resisters League is a pacifist organization that views all wars as crimes against humanity. It challenges military recruitment, sees profiteering as a primary motivation for armed conflict, organizes nonviolent direct action, and seeks to address the causes of war directly through advocacy and activism.

Bibliography

Books

Tanya Biank — *Under the Sabers: The Unwritten Code of Army Wives.* New York: St. Martin's Press, 2006.

Penny Coleman — *Flashback; Posttraumatic Stress Disorder, Suicide, and the Lessons of War.* Boston, MA: Beacon Press, 2006.

Christopher P. Coppola — *A Pediatric Surgeon in Iraq.* Chicago, IL: NTI Upstream, 2009.

Patricia P. Driscoll and Celia Straus — *Hidden Battles on Unseen Fronts: Stories of American Soldiers with Traumatic Brain Injury and PTSD.* Drexel Hill, PA: Casemate, 2009.

Aaron Glantz — *The War Comes Home: Washington's Battle Against America's Veterans.* Berkeley: University of California Press, 2009.

Dave Grossman — *On Killing: The Psychological Cost of Learning to Kill in War and Society.* New York: Little, Brown and Co., 2009.

Katharine Hall and Dale Stahl — *An Argument for Documenting Casualties: Violence Against Iraqi Civilians 2006.* Santa Monica, CA: Rand, 2008.

Peter J. Hoffman and Thomas George Weiss

Sword and Salve: Confronting New Wars and Humanitarian Crises. Lanham, MD: Rowman & Littlefield, 2006.

P.R. Kumaraswamy

Caught in Crossfire: Civilians in Conflicts in the Middle East. Reading, NY: Ithaca Press, 2008.

Melissa Larner, James Peto, and Nadine Käthe Monem

War and Medicine. London: Black Dog, 2008.

Eric V. Larson and Bogdan Savych

Misfortunes of War: Press and Public Reactions to Civilian Deaths in Wartime. Santa Monica, CA: Rand, 2007.

Ilona Meagher

Moving a Nation to Care: Post-Traumatic Stress Disorder and America's Returning Troops. Brooklyn, NY: Ig Publishing, 2007.

Victor Montgomery, III

Healing Suicidal Veterans: Recognizing, Supporting and Answering Their Pleas for Help. Far Hills, NJ: New Horizon Press, 2009.

Don Philpott and Janelle Hill

The Wounded Warrior Handbook: A Resource Guide for Returning Veterans. Lanham, MD: Government Institutes, 2009.

Martin Schram

Vets Under Siege: How America Deceives and Dishonors Those Who Fight Our Battles. New York: Thomas Dunne Books, 2008.

Nancy Sherman	*Stoic Warriors: The Ancient Philosophy Behind the Military Mind.* New York: Oxford University Press, 2005.
Nancy Sherman	*The Untold War: Inside the Hearts, Minds and Souls of our Soldiers.* New York: W.W. Norton, 2010.
David Livingston Smith	*The Most Dangerous Animal: Human Nature and the Origins of War.* New York: St. Martin's Press, 2007.
Terri Tanielian and Lisa H Jaycox, eds.	*Invisible Wounds of War: Psychological and Cognitive Injuries, Their Consequences, and Services to Assist Recovery.* Santa Monica, CA: Rand, 2008.

Periodicals and Internet Sources

Michael A. Cohen	"The Myth of a Kinder, Gentler War," *World Policy Journal*, April, 2010.
Noam Cohen	"Through Soldiers' Eyes, 'The First YouTube War,'" *New York Times*, May 24, 2010.
Yochi J. Dreazen	"Gates Says Civilian Deaths Test War Strategy," *Wall Street Journal*, April 14, 2010.
Bob Egelko	"Veterans Not Entitled to Mental Health Care, U.S. Lawyers Argue," *San Francisco Chronicle*, February 5, 2008.

Carlotta Gall and David E. Sanger	"Civilian Deaths Undermine War on Taliban," *New York Times*, May 12, 2007.
Lourdes Garcia-Navarro	"Bitterness Grows Amid U.S.-Backed Sons of Iraq," *NPR*, June 24, 2010.
Don Gonyea	"Ban on Media Coverage of Military Coffins Revisited," *NPR*, February 11, 2009
Nick Hewitt	"Return of the Fallen," *History Today*, September, 2009.
Mark Hosenball	"The Drone Dilemma," *Newsweek*, December 21, 2009.
Paul Krugman	"Health Care Confidential," *New York Times*, January 27, 2006.
Michelle Lore	"Defending Iraq War Vets," *St. Paul Legal Ledger*, July 12, 2007.
Colman McCarthy	"Stories of Dead Civilians Will Never Get a Hearing," *National Catholic Reporter*, June 11, 2010.
Brian Mockenhaupt	"The Doctor's War," *Atlantic Monthly*, October, 2009.
Sharon Otterman	"Civilian Toll Rising in Afghanistan, U.N. Says," *New York Times*, July 31, 2009.
Michael M. Phillips	"Civilians in Cross Hairs Slow Troops," *Wall Street Journal*, February 22, 2010.

George W. Reilly   "More Female Veterans Turning to
                       VA Centers for Health Care,"
                       Providence Journal, April 24, 2006.

Connie Schultz   "Let Cameras Record the Sad
                       Homecomings of the Fallen,"
                       Cleveland Plain Dealer, February 18,
                       2009.

Jonathan Steele   "Iraq's Civilian Dead: Why US Won't
and Suzanne   Do the Maths," *Sydney Morning
Goldenberg   Herald*, March 21, 2008.

Christian Toto   "From War, Lives are Saved: Combat
                       Injuries Lead to Rapid Medical
                       Advances," *Washington Times*, May
                       22, 2007.

Bob Woodruff   "'Something was Different.' Vet Copes
and Jim Hill   with Invisible Injury," *ABC News*,
                       March 7, 2007.

Hope Yen   "Commission on Veterans Care
                       Pledges to Develop Solutions,"
                       Washington Post, April 15, 2007.

Index

Numerals

9/11, 75, 101, 103, 105–106
  commission, 68

A

Abdulmutallab, Umar Farouk, 99
Adams, Brad, 25, 26
Aeromedical evacuation teams
  (AETs), 60
Afghan National Army, 28
Afghanistan, 8, 14, 16–24, 56, 61,
  64–65, 70–71, 75, 81
    Azizabad, 25
    Kabul, 19
    Shindad District, 27
Agent Orange, 67
Alaska, 76, 84
    Anchorage, 82
    East Anchorage, 76
    Fairbanks, 77
Alaska Suicide Prevention Coun-
  cil, 82
Ali, Marie, 46
al–Jaafri, Ibrahim, 61
al Qaeda, 20, 26, 102, 103
American Cancer Society, 99
American Foundation for Suicide
  Prevention, 90
American International Group
  (AIG), 40, 46
Anan 7, 12
Arabian Peninsula, 102
Arlington National Cemetery, 48
Arlington, Texas, 45
Armstrong, Col. Joel, 45

Army. *See U.S. Army*
Army Bases. See U.S. Military
  Bases
Army Suicide Prevention Task-
  force, 71
Army Times (newspaper), 66
Asia, 97
Associated Press (AP), 49, 52–53

B

Baghdad, 13
Begich, Mark, 82
Bilmes, Linda, 61–64, 67–68
Bradley fighting vehicles, 66
Brigade combat team, 76
Brooke Army Medical Center, 17
Burial services
    media coverage of, 47–59
    memorial service, 76, 78
    military burial/honors, 48, 74,
    76
Burton, Dan, 89
Bush administration, 52, 64, 103,
  106
    See also Bush, George W.
Byrnes, Pvt. 1st Class Edward, 84

C

Cassidy, Sgt. Gerald, 17
Casualties of war, 7, 11
    civilian casualties, 24–27
    Fort Hood shooting, 16
    military casualties, 16, 29–32
    See also Wounded soldiers

Centers for Disease Control and Prevention (CDC), 98–99
Central Point, OR, 34
Central Valley, CA, 18
Chapman, Sgt. Joseph, 49
Chemical warfare, 68
    anti–anthrax injections, 68
Chiarelli, Gen. Peter, 81
China, 97
Christianity, 91
    canonical law, 92
    Christmas Day, 99
Civilian workers, 24, 35–36
    contract workers, 35
    interpreters, 43
    See also Casualties of war
Clancy, Tom, 37
Cognitive difficulties, 7
Cold War, 102
Columbia University, 61
Congressional Budget Office, 62
Constitution, 21
    constitutional convention, 21
Continental Airlines, 99
craigslist, 57
Critical care air transport (CCAT), 60
Cumberland River Center Pavilion, 18

D

Davenport, IA, 48
Defense and Veterans Brain Injury Center, 8
Defense Base Act, 40, 42, 46
Democracy, 22
Department of Defense, 9, 10, 16, 31, 49, 52, 54, 72

Department of Homeland Security, 102
Detroit, MI, 99
DynCorp International, 36

E

E. coli bacteria, 100
Eastasia, 15
eBay, 57
Eminiar VII, 11, 12
England, 92
Entertainment Tonight (TV program), 57
Eurasia, 15

F

Facebook, 90
Federal Bureau of Investigations (FBI), 98
Fish, Spc. John, 17
Florida, 14
Founding fathers, 21
Franklin, Benjamin, 21
Frederikson, Lee, 36
Freedom of Information Act (FOIA), 53–55

G

Gaestel, Pvt. Tim, 78–80
Gates, Robert, 49, 53–54
Germany, 38
Glasgow International Airport, 99
Grant Pass, OR, 37
Gregg, Jim, 41
Grenada, 14
Griffis, Lacy, 83–85
Griffis, Spec. Steven, 83–85
Gulf War, 13, 64–65

H

Hadi, Maleq, 45
Ham, Gen. Carter, 81
Hardy, Warren, 7
Hawaii, 82
Hawkins, Roger, 40
Hoge, Dr. Charles W., 9
Hopewell, VA, 48
Houston, TX, 39
Howard, Col. Michael, 81
Hudson River, 99
Hum vees, 66, 83
Human Rights Watch, 24, 25, 26, 27, 28
Hurd, Jason, 38
Hussein, Saddam, 13

I

I Love Lucy (TV series), 14
icasualties.org, 17
Improvised Explosive Devices (IEDs), 7, 19
India, 97
Institute for Rehabilitation and Research (TIRR), 39
International Security Assistance Force (ISAF), 19, 28
Iraq, 7, 14–18, 30–32, 48, 61, 64, 70–71, 75, 83, 88–89
    Fallujah, 18
    Mosul, 81
    Tikrit, 7
Iraq War, 8, 29, 33, 37
    Operation Iraqi Freedom, 30
Islam
    muslims, 92
Israel, 97

J

Jackson, Michael, 56–58
Joint Chiefs of Staff, 71
Jordan, 44

K

Karzai, Hamid, 28
KBR Inc., 37, 39
Keesling, Gregg, 88
Kennedy, Patrick, 89
Kirk, James T. *See* Shatner, William
Korea, 14, 64
Kothari, Dr. Sunil, 39

L

Lane, Linda, 34–42
Lane, Reggie, 34–42
Lanese, Herbert J., 36
Lebanon Junction, Kentucky, 49
Lee, Robert E., 11
Limerick, Ireland, 84
Lindsey, Larry, 62, 67
Little Rock, AR, 101
Lobbyists, 102, 106
Los Angeles, CA, 56
Los Angeles Times (newspaper), 44, 45, 63

M

M1 Abram tanks, 66
M113 armored personnel carriers, 66
Marshall Plan, 68
Martyrdom, 92
Medal of Honor, 96
Melnyk, Lt. Col. Les, 48

Middle East, 33, 68
Military. See U.S. Military
Military draft, 22
Mission Critical Psychological Services, 36
Moore, Brenda, 82
Mount, Judson E., 17
Mr. Spock. *See* Nimoy, Leonard
Mullen, Admiral Mike, 71
Murphy, Frances, 65
Myers, Staff Sgt. Phillip A., 48

N

National Atlantic Treaty Organization (NATO), 24, 25, 26, 28
National Weather Service, 99
Nazi Germany, 102
New England Journal of Medicine (journal), 9
New York Times (*NY Times*) (newspaper), 88, 104–105
New Yorker (magazine), 105
Nigeria
    Nigerian, 102
Nightline (TV program), 7
Nimoy, Leonard, 12
Nobel laureate, 61
North Carolina, 18
Northwest Airlines, 99

O

Obama administration, 20, 74, 93, 100, 103, 105. *See also*Obama, Barack.
Orange County, CA, 103

P

Pakistan, 14, 57
Panama, 14

Paris, 99
Paso Robles, CA, 17
Pautsch, David, 48, 50
Pentagon, 8, 17, 43, 46–48, 51–54, 60, 63–64, 70, 72
Persian Gulf War, 48
Pew Research Center
    Project for Excellence, 100
Philadelphia, 21
Philbrick, Col. Christopher, 71
Post–Traumatic Stress Disorder (PTSD), 18, 66, 82–83, 89, 92, 96
Presidents
    Bush, George H. W., 13, 48, 52
    Bush, George W., 14, 61, 66, 68, 101, 104–105
    Kennedy, John F., 103
    Nixon, Richard, 104
    Obama, Barack, 16, 88–89, 93, 103
ProPublica, 8, 44
PsychiatryTalk.com, 88

R

Rand, Sgt. Brian Jason, 18
Raya, Andes, 18
Refugees, 44
Republic, 22
Republican Party (GOP), 95, 100, 104
Rio de Janeiro, 99
Ritchie, Col. Elspeth, 73
Rivas, Lt. Col. Raymond, 83
Rocket propelled grenade, 38
Rogers, Hal, 74
Rules of engagement, 28
Rumsfeld, Donald, 62, 66, 103
Russia, 97

Soviet Russia, 102

S

San Antonio, 17
Schloesser, Maj. Gen. Jeffrey, 72
Schmachtenberger, Staff Sgt. Anthony, 75, 77–78
Senate Armed Services Committee, 82
September 11, 2001. *See 9/11*
Sharpton, Al, 57
Shatner, William, 11–12, 15
Simpson, O. J., 103
Skold, Brian William, 18
Social Security, 95
Soldiers. *See U.S. Troops*
Somalia, 14
Star Trek (TV series), 11, 15
Stiglitz, Joseph, 61, 64, 66
Suicide, 92–93
    military response, 70, 75, 81
    Presidential letter of condolence, 74, 87, 89, 91–92
    soldier suicide, 70, 71, 77, 87–89
    suicide bombings, 25
    suicide taskforce, 73
Swine flu, 98

T

Taliban, 20, 25, 26, 28
Terrorism, 97, 98, 101
    war on terror, 94, 102–103, 105
Traumatic Brain Injury (TBI), 7, 8, 82
Troy, Maj. Gen. William, 76, 78, 81

U

United States, 97–98
Unmanned drones, 13
U.S. Air Force, 48
    82nd Airborne, 75, 78, 80
    101st Airborne Division, 72
    Air Force Mortuary Affairs Office, 49
    Andrews Air Force Base, 69
    Dover Air Force Base (Dover AFB), 48, 49, 51, 53–55
US Airways, 99
U.S. Army, 14, 18, 31, 44, 46, 70, 82
    1st Battalion, 78
    2nd Battalion, 79
    864th Engineer Combat Battalion, 83
    Centcom, 62
    First Armored Division, 7
    Marine Corps, 18, 20
    Military Police (MPs), 85
    Military Reserves, 31
    National Guard, 31, 77
    Office of the Army Surgeon General, 73
    U.S. troops, 19, 22, 25, 26, 29–33, 47, 53–58, 61–62
U.S. Military bases
    Fort Bragg, 75, 78
    Fort Campbell, 18, 72, 73
    Fort Hood, 16, 17
    Fort Knox, 17
    Fort Rich, 77–79, 81, 84
    Fort Richardson, 75–76, 83
    Fort Wainwright, 77–78
U.S. taxpayers, 61

V

Varney, Joe, 73
Veterans, 8, 17, 94, 97
    Department of Veterans Affairs, 40, 63, 95, 97
    Veterans Administration, 9, 10, 64–65, 68, 72, 95
    Veterans Affairs Committee, 82
Vietnam, 12, 31, 64, 67, 94, 104
    North Vietnam, 30
    South Vietnam, 30
    Vietnam War, 29, 30
Virginia Tech University, 101
Virtual Behavioral Health Pilot Program, 81
Voss, Justin, 85

W

Wall Street Journal (newspaper), 67
Walter Reed Army Institute, 9, 66
    Division of Psychiatry and Neuroscience, 9
    Walter Reed Army Medical Center, 61
Walters, Barbara, 58

War, 14, 15, 101
Washington, DC, 21, 53
Washington Post (newspaper), 53, 63, 66
West Palm Beach, FL, 83
White House, 62, 67
Whitman, Bryan, 54–55
Wichita Falls, TX, 84
Winkenwerger, Dr. William, 63
Wolfowitz, Paul, 62
Woodruff, Bob, 7
Woods, Christie, 49
Woods, Staff Sgt. Gary L., 49
World War I, 64
World War II, 46
Wounded soldiers, 61–69
    care of, 60
    cost of medical care, 61–69; 94–97
    emotional impact, 72–74
    See also Casualties of war
    See also Suicide

Y

Yemen, 98, 102, 105
Yugoslavia, 14